Occupying Aging

Delights, Disabilities, and Daily Life

Katherine Schneider

First published by Dog Ear Publishing
4010 W. 86th Street, Ste H
Indianapolis, IN 46268
www.dogearpublishing.net

ISBN: 978-1-4575-2320-5

This book is printed on acid-free paper.

Printed in the United States of America

My head is bloody, but unbowed.
I am the master of my fate,
I am the captain of my soul.

> — Invictus; by William Ernest Henley

Hope smiles on the threshold of the year to come, whispering that it will be happier.

> —Alfred, Lord Tennyson

For all that has been, thanks; to all that will be, yes.

> —Dag Hammarskjöld

Introduction

Why Read this Book

Perhaps you're one of the forty million Americans over sixty-five or the 76 million Americans called baby boomers who are joining the over sixty-five set at a rate of 8,000 per day. I'm one of you and would love to take you on a ride with me through a full year of occupying aging. I've been blind since birth and have had fibromyalgia for over twenty years, so I've struggled with disabilities and society's disabling attitudes long enough to have learned a few tricks of the trade. As you'll see if you tag along, sometimes they work and sometimes...I'm not sure who first said "if it doesn't kill you, it'll make you stronger" but I could have that as my motto.

The year is full of delightful people and events, as well as tears and laughter. The other major characters in this journal are my Seeing Eye dogs past and present. They'd encourage you to read the book because then at least some good will come of my spending so much time tapping on the keyboard of my talking computer.

Welcome to my year of occupying aging. I hope it encourages you in occupying your life at whatever stage in the journey of life you are.

January 1: Beginning Occupying and Resolutions

What's it like being old? A few intrepid children actually ask me that when I'm giving talks on blindness/disability in elementary schools. Then there are the 50-somethings who want to know "what's retirement like?" Their voices hold some balance between the suppressed excitement of waiting for Christmas when you're little and the anxiety of "Can I afford this house?" of the first-time home buyer.

Since I'm writing this during a leap year, this book will offer 366 answers to these wonderings. But it's also a pick your own adventure book, so if July 3rd's entry fits for you better on February 15, go for it! Occupying aging is done one person at a time as well as one day at a time.

I don't often make New Year's resolutions, but this year some gentle resolves came to mind. I want more prayer, more poetry, and more success with puzzles in my life. Being a book-a-holic, I've already gathered several books on each topic. That's the easy part! Will I actually choose to read and reflect on them? There are three hundred sixty-five days left this year for that question to be answered.

January 2: Occupying an Aging Body. Ads

Today's e-mail brought a nice story about Target using a picture of a child with Down's syndrome in their clothing ad. For those of us with visible disabilities, this represents a victory that doesn't happen often enough—a victory of being seen as normal. Not courageous, not special, just normal. The same issue comes up for the aged. Sleek, non-disabled aging may appear occasionally in ads, but not the real thing with lumps, bumps, and scars carrying their oxygen tank on their walker.

Before starting a petition drive to our favorite television network or magazine to use real photos instead of digitally enhanced images, we may have to do some internal work. Nora Ephron's humorous reflections in *I Feel Bad about My Neck* represent many of our internal dialogues about our bodies. Since I've been blind from birth, I've had time to adjust to that physical imperfection, but the sags and creaks of aging are new. If it still works, I can celebrate that. Then there's the "it's been part of me for this long so it deserves some respect" line. Occupying an aging body takes more than a day—maybe a lifetime.

January 3: Special Diets and Special Needs

Cooking supper for some friends, one of whom is a brittle diabetic, makes me think about all the little adjustments we make or don't for each other's differences. I'm a vegetarian, so no meat on the menu, other than fish or shrimp, which I'll eat on special occasions—where two or three are gathered together, it's special. Protein is good and fish is brain food which is important for the game of bridge that will follow the meal.

My friend has already pointed out the basics of cooking for any special diet: if it tastes good, you can't have it! There will be a shrimp cocktail for protein, ravioli in V8 juice for the starch, slaw (a vegetable chewable by a guest with false teeth) and stewed apples for dessert. With a little apple pie spice on them, you can imagine the pie without the carbs. For me, it's an occasional exercise in considering others' dietary needs, for the diabetic's spouse it's a daily concern. Should she have high-carb stuff she enjoys around the house or not? Yes, he's in charge of his diabetic control, but out of sight might help with out of mind. But if she goes without too many times, and she's built anything like I am, resentment may ensue.

I've experienced this dilemma from the other side when sighted people talk about experiences like going to an art show of paintings that I can't enjoy. After about ninety seconds of being interested in knowing about it enough to be able to mention it to other friends who might enjoy it, I'm ready for the conversation to move to a different topic. If I can't have it, I don't want to dwell on it.

Balancing my desire to have chocolate for dessert after the apples, I briefly brought out the Christmas box of chocolates to pass. The diabetic passed on them and I put the box away after passing it around once. Hopefully, all at the dinner knew it was cooked and served with love, which has no carbs.

January 4: Celebrating Louis Braille's Birthday

What did you do to celebrate Louis Braille's birthday? I wrote a summary of the activities of a National Library Service for the Blind committee that I serve on. Then I started work on an article for a local aging agency's newsletter on our library's services of particular interest to people with low vision.

Louis Braille's birthday certainly deserves celebrating. In the early 1800s he developed a system that enabled people who are blind to be independent readers.

Many seniors whose vision deteriorates to the point where they can't read even large print do not learn Braille. It's hard to learn especially if you have neuropathy, but it is useful for making notes, jotting down phone numbers, and playing cards. Tape recorders and talking computers can do a lot, but Mr. Braille's invention will always be useful to those of us who have learned the code. It's amazing that six dots can represent mathematical symbols, musical notes, Chinese characters, and English letters. There are not Braille equivalents of emoticons that I know of, but that may come someday.

If you're not a Braille reader and don't happen to know anyone who is, you can still celebrate the day. Run your fingers over the Braille numbers in the next elevator you're on and think about how you'd know what button to push if you couldn't see. Next time you're in a big hotel, imagine jumping off the elevator on a random floor and trying your key card in the third door down a number of times until you get the right floor.

Next week when I get to read Scripture at church I will thank God for Louis Braille's birth and for his blindness which prompted his invention. If that hadn't happened, I'd have to memorize the readings in order to declaim them and with this aging brain that would be a lot of work.

January 5: Taking Help and Giving Help

Greeting at our local soup kitchen, The Community Table, and delivering pet food and supplies to elderly and disabled pet owners this week reminded me to be grateful for my food and my Seeing Eye dog, Fran's food as well. I was employed for thirty years, so in retirement I can afford to buy decent food for myself and also the allergy dog food

Fran needs. I have friends with cars who are willing to take me shopping once a month or pick up that occasional item I forget and just must have. This week the must have item was toilet paper. Without thinking through all the implications of it, I volunteered to host a political worker in town for two weeks. I then realized that with two people answering the call of nature at my house the two rolls left might not last until my next shopping trip.

When you have disabilities, you learn to be more organized and planful. I noticed this with a friend who uses a walker with a basket for her stuff instead of a shoulder bag. She had to direct another friend in how to disassemble the walker, put it in the trunk, and put the basket in just so, so the contents didn't spill. The job got done and the lunch was enjoyed; it just took a bit of extra time and planning.

Just like for the people who come to the Community Table for their daily meal, or the elders in the pet food program, the need for sustenance is met. As did many people on the pet food route, I say thank you to a community that will take the extra time and energy to meet my needs individually and respectfully.

January 6: Letter to a Young Friend

Today I wrote a letter. Yes, an actual letter — not an e-mail! It involved two of my New Year's resolves; prayer and puzzles. I was writing to a youngster I know whose cancer has recently been diagnosed as stage 4 (the most aggressive). Since she's recovering from surgery and not at school at the moment, I decided, after prayerful consideration of what I could do to make her world better, that I'd become her weekly pen pal. I wanted my letter to represent my caring but not be too serious. I included a riddle along with a question or two about her rehab and daily activities. Maybe just the right poem will cross my path to include in next week's letter so I can cover all my resolves.

Would I have taken time to do this while I was working? I would have tried to slap something together but I couldn't have browsed through twenty riddles to find just the right one, like I did. And it would have seemed like a chore instead of a fun challenge to be looking for tidbits for future letters.

January 7: Slowing Down in Winter and Life

As Hoagy Carmichael said: "Slow motion gets you there faster." I chafe at this, but in many cases it's true. I was out for a walk this morning and, even though it's a mild winter, we're blessed with patchy ice. My Seeing Eye dog is very conscientious about ice, so she stops when she gets to a patch to figure out how best to get me through it. Sometimes she needs to snug up against my leg and just go slowly forward; sometimes she's better off walking on the edge of the grass so at least she has firm footing. If I push her to go, go, go too quickly, my haste may land me on my behind. Even though it's well padded, it hurts and the hurt hangs around longer when you're aged. Also, it really upsets my dog, who takes personal responsibility for it even though I was the one pushing her. I've seen her walk an extra block to avoid a patch of ground where I've fallen. Slowing down, taking a deep breath, and humming "Slow down, you're going too fast…You've got to make the moment last" is the better way, whether we're talking icy sidewalks or LIFE.

January 8: Epiphany and Epiphanies

In the church year, today is Epiphany. One of the things I love about retirement is the little epiphanies I have. I'm taking the time to notice the little things more often: the good feeling of the warmth from the sun, the beautiful horn concerto on public radio as I exercise, and the fun of a game of chase with Fran with her new toy. These same things happened before retirement, but I didn't take the time to notice them and savor them. If you want to practice for retirement, try savoring a sight, a smell, a feeling, or a sound instead of just noticing it and jumping on to the next thing. Whether you call it mindfulness or joy in the moment, it doesn't cost anything and it probably burns calories, so go ahead and try it!

January 9: Saying "no"

Can I say "no" without guilt? Back when I worked as a psychologist, I taught assertiveness and often recommended *When I Say No, I Feel Guilty.* I did agree with clients that it was easier said than done. This is particularly true for women, the aged, the disabled, and anyone else who is worried that they might not be asked or included again if they say "no" this time. My current case in point involves having the guts to say I'll attend a meeting by phone in Madison instead of in person. If I go in person, I'll spend twice as long riding to and from as I'll spend in the meeting, to say nothing of hunting around for a ride. The thought "What will people think?" competes with I want to be home in time for Friday night's bridge game. Hey, I'm retired—count me in for the bridge game!

After all the agonizing, I e-mailed the gal in charge of the meeting and asked if she could arrange for me to phone in. "Sure," she e-mailed back. When will I learn?

January 10: Mentors for *Occupying Aging*

Right after I retired, I joined a morning reading group at a friend's Methodist church. Church ladies who read are my kind of people. The average age of the group is around eighty, so I figured I could learn a few things about aging with grace and style. I've learned to slow down and to laugh with someone when they can't remember, say a non sequitur because they didn't hear right, fall asleep during the meeting, and jerk awake. As the years have flown by, we've lost a few members by death and moves to nursing homes. Others can't put the energy into reading and reviewing a book or don't see well enough to read their own notes so we've figured out other reading-related activities. February is poetry circle and those who don't bring a poem to read pull one out of their memory and declaim it to us. These women show care and compassion to each other, which truly inspires me. Originally, they let me join because of my friend and because of my cute dog, but they've come to value my ideas for work-arounds when eyesight fails. Today I'll take my digital talking book player and play a little segment from a church humor book.

They are so down to earth about the nuisances of lugging around a walker; having to go to the bathroom more often, and not remembering the title of the book they just read and wanted to tell us about. They laugh and move on. They, and authors like May Sarton, are my mentors for occupying aging.

January 11: Savoring Ordinary Time

Even going out to lunch is different in retirement. If the service is slow, no problem, because this was the main event today. There was time to really talk with friends, discuss books, and hear workplace gossip from the two members of the lunch party who were still working. I haven't slowed down my eating yet, so I am done in time to get back to work, but that will come with time and practice I'm sure.

In the church year, the Christmas season is done and we're in Ordinary Time. Part of retirement is for savoring the ordinary, like lunch with friends. Too bad I didn't do it more often before retiring. Savoring wouldn't have taken any more time than rushing through, but everybody else was rushing, so I did too. Now I can smile when people tell me how busy they are and be glad I don't have to compete in the busyness Olympics.

January 12: Beautiful Snowy Day

What should I do with my busy "monkey mind," as the Buddhists call it, while I shovel? One can never have too much beauty in one's life, so I'm focusing on all the sensory beauty I can: a crow claiming territory or celebrating the day (it's hard to tell); squirrels chattering their complaints at nuts being covered up; the muffled sounds of traffic; soft, light, fluffy snow: beautiful classical music on the radio when I go inside; hot coffee to warm up with; and the little bit of warmth from the sun.

Let's try a haiku or two to celebrate the beauty:

Soft and fluffy snow
Makes shoveling something more
Than a job—a joy?

Later in the day:
Mildly aching back
A least it can still bend and
Lift the damn shovel.

January 13: Friday the Thirteenth and Luck

I could tell right away that it was Friday the thirteenth. . I managed to put too much milk in the scrambled eggs and overfill a coffee cup. Is that whole Friday the thirteenth thing just superstition?

But, honestly, I feel so lucky in so many ways, I can handle runny eggs. I was born lucky. In 1949, when I was born, they knew to give premature infants oxygen to keep them alive. Years later they figured out how to not give them so much so they weren't blinded. I was lucky to grow up in a family that valued education and pushed me to achieve. Without that I wouldn't have had my challenging and interesting thirty-year career as a psychologist. I was lucky to be able to retire while I was reasonably healthy and energetic. Picking my own adventures each day is a privilege.

So bring it on, Friday the thirteenth I'm a lucky woman anyway!

January 14: Games

Fresh from a drubbing at bridge last night, I'm mulling over what makes games so fun. Card games like whist, the forerunner of bridge, date back to the sixteenth century, so the appeal is not new to modern man. Of course, there's the new wrinkle of playing on an electronic device, no human interaction necessary. My friends who do this, however, consider it far inferior to sitting down with friends.

There's the intellectual challenge of bridge, Sudoku or whatever game you prefer. As we're aging, we're encouraged to keep our brains in working order by playing games. No more should we heed that voice in the back of our heads from childhood asking: "Don't you have something better to do?" We're licensed to play.
There's also the social part of playing a game. You can psychologize about who will do what in a given situation—will she really shoot the moon in hearts? Of course, there's always the news/gossip that other players bring to keep your mind active, or at least your tongue wagging.

No wonder our animal companions, of the four footed variety, anyway also enjoy games. Tug of war for my guide dog after a painstaking walk on ice relieves stress, gives her attention, and lets her strategize just for fun. I wonder if she could solve that Sudoku for me!

January 15: Recalculating

Several of my older friends are coping with new health issues. Yearly doctor visits have become quarterly, tests done, diagnoses made, and adjustments begun.

When my talking GPS gets annoyed because I take a different route than it suggests, it says "recalculating." That's what my friends are doing. They are recalculating how they're going to tackle daily life activities with diminished energy, loss of skills and abilities, and figuring out new strategies. Counting carbs and grams of salt can turn a sweep through the grocery store to grab a few things into a label-reading, day-long expedition. The same kinds of calculations go into energy expenditures for some. If I shovel the walk, will I still feel like walking the dog? Should I hire a house-cleaner, or spend that money on fun things?

Then there's the recalculating about what to tell whom. For reasons I cannot fathom, low vision and cancer seem to elicit better responses from people than hearing difficulties, diabetes, and memory issues. Helpful responses include: "I'm sorry to hear that and how can I help?" Less helpful routinely include: "I know someone who died of that"; "you shouldn't have smoked or eaten birthday cake"; and "you must go to Mexico for treatment, learn to meditate, and do just what my third cousin did."

When my GPS recalculates, it issues a low hiss to let me know it isn't pleased. As my friends recalculate to their new health issues, there's plenty of hissing too. Because I've been blind since birth, I understand the frustrations of learning to do things differently and deal with other peoples' reactions. I can listen empathically to their hissing and occasionally add a story of my own.

January 16: Martin Luther King Jr. Day

On Martin Luther King Jr. Day, I am thinking about how I can become more like him in nonviolent confrontation of discrimination. In theory, I understand and agree with his view that only love can drive out hate, but when someone steps on the civil rights of someone I care about, I get angry and want to pound them. With a few deep breaths, I can usually muster a firm but polite response, but I'm not feeling love toward them.

The most memorable teaching I've had on this subject was from a supervisor at my internship at Central Louisiana State Hospital. She would respond to my sputtering indignation about injustices I observed by pointing out that honey attracts more flies than vinegar. A few times I got to observe her applying honey to a situation and saw that it worked. Gradually, I tried it and found it worked more often than getting in someone's face with "it's the law" without any acknowledgment of their humanity first. One incident I remember was a motel trying to charge me $50 extra, because I had a guide dog, they'd "have to vacuum after I left." Apparently, they didn't otherwise, which made me wish I hadn't stayed there, but that was water over the bridge. "That's illegal," was almost out of my mouth when I thought to say, "I'll bet you know that's not legal, don't you?" To which they responded, "Well I wasn't sure," and took it off the bill.

This quote from Dr. King helps me focus on the starting point for my nonviolent action, me.

"The nonviolent approach does not immediately change the heart of the oppressor. It first does something to the hearts and souls of those committed to it. It gives them new self-respect; it calls up resources of strength and courage they did not know they had."

I'll pray to be more loving in the agape sense of love, not the mushy sense.

January 17: Being an Encourager

When I retired I thought a lot about the kinds of volunteer work I'd like to do. Because of licensing issues, like the fact that it costs several hundred dollars a year to remain licensed, I decided not to volunteer anywhere as a psychologist. But with no license necessary, I decided I could become an encourager. So I've had fun figuring out how to do this with friends and people I do business with.

Today for example, someone was trying to help me with a computer issue and we were getting nowhere fast. I ended the conversation with "Thanks for trying and let me know what you find out, will you?" Being much younger than me, her response was "No problem. I'll let you know what I find out." I don't understand the "no problem" because we both know there is one, but that is twenty-something speak for "Have a nice day!" I think.

Other encouraging efforts for today include; sending a real letter to a friend with cancer, forwarding interesting articles/jokes, making a phone call, e-mailing "good job" fan mail to someone I saw perform in a program last night, and preparing for book club so I can encourage the leader by being an active discussant.

I grew up in a family that thought if you told people what they were doing wrong, that was all you needed to say. I have had to learn encouraging skills as an adult. My most memorable lesson was from my first Seeing Eye dog. One August afternoon we were walking to work and I was crabbing at her to hurry up. She slowed down and I crabbed more. Eventually she stopped and sat down on her Labrador rump. I crabbed louder. Finally I realized I had to do something different. I started talking nicely about how hot I knew she was and how if we could ease on over to work, it would be air-conditioned there. We did and my encourager skills began to grow.

In retirement I find it encouraging to be extremely useful. I don't have the power to get what I want done because the person works for me or wants a grade from me. Encouraging is free, it's fun, and it works! As we waddled off for today's short exercise walk in subzero temperatures, I whistled a happy tune to encourage myself. Fran has not expressed her opinion on whether my whistling is an encourager or a discourager. When we return, I'll have rutabagas a friend shared with me, no doubt to encourage me to eat more cruciferous vegetables. I'm lucky to know many encouragers to model my efforts on.

January 18: Staying Fit Your Way

Someone on a LISTSERV of blind people wrote today about being denied service by a fitness center she wanted to join. They seemed to think she'd need more help than they had time to give and maybe get in other people's way and be an insurance risk.

Other members of the list had a variety of good solutions, from talking to the manager, threatening a letter to the editor of the local paper, and threatening a lawsuit if all else failed. I contributed my solution of buying weights and hiring a personal trainer for a couple of sessions to show me how to safely use them.

I don't know if it is wisdom, tiredness, or what, but as I age I find myself picking my battles more carefully. Thirty years ago I bet I would have said "That's wrong, let's tango." Nowadays there's more consideration of what my goal is and how else I can achieve it. If I want to get fit, what's easiest for me? I enjoyed the one-to-one instruction and the comfort of my own environment with no technology hassles. Amazingly though, I still find the same "no time" excuse that people who go to the gym give for breaking their New Year's resolutions.

January 19: Being a Mentor

I recently agreed to mentor a blind college student who wants a career in a field similar to mine. Often retired friends are also involved in various kinds of mentoring. Several of us were talking about what we have to offer. Many times the fields we worked in and the technologies have changed a lot. We can listen and encourage and we can offer people skills like networking and manners.

As I think back on supervisors and bosses who have mentored me over the years, the biggest gift they gave me was believing in me. I remember several times when knowing they liked and believed in me gave me the courage to admit wrong moves I'd made and look for better ways to handle a situation next time. I've never had a blind mentor, so that will be another level of complexity this student and I will have to work out. How much help one asks for, whether one uses a dog or cane, and reads Braille or not, is such an individual choice.

In the past I've loved mentoring young psychologists and I still hear from some of them. I also feel like a proud aunt when I hear back from students who have read to me as a job. That's such an intense one-to-one employment situation because I trust them to write checks and read mail. A strong bond often ensues. This Christmas my current student reader was really amazed to read me Christmas letters from a gal who read to me thirty years ago. Somehow I don't know if friending on Facebook will work as well for keeping the mentor/mentee bond over the years as the much-maligned Christmas letter.

January 20: Accessible Voting

An organization I'm part of wasn't providing accessible voting for all its members and I jumped to the barricades with more energy than I knew I had. The organization is a private voluntary organization, so accessible voting is not a legal matter, just moral. After I made my impassioned speech and suggested a way to do it, there were no questions and no disagreement. I can easily start to wonder what they were thinking and get mad. Instead, I try to ask myself "did I do what I needed to do in the most positive way possible?" I think I get an A minus.

In 2006, when I got a secret ballot for the first time in my life, I cried. It's so tied up with what it means to me to be an American. Before that I had to have a friend or two poll officials, one from each party, help me vote. Now every polling place in the country must have a "handicapped" voting machine. You use a remote to mark your ballot and hear the choices read through earphones. You can even do a write-in candidate.

January 21: Squirrel Appreciation Day

Today is Squirrel Appreciation Day! It turns out the day was started in 2001 by a wildlife rehabilitator. It can best be celebrated by leaving some food out for them or just watching and enjoying their antics.

There are 200 species of squirrels on every continent except Australia and Antarctica. A group of these rodents is called a "scurry." Their front teeth grow six inches per year—the better to gnaw with. Anyone who has tried to keep them out of a bird feeder knows they're smart and determined. I didn't know that sometimes they'll gnaw a rattlesnake's skin and then daub the smell on themselves to discourage scent-driven predators.

Maybe I could celebrate by eating some nuts myself. Go nuts and celebrate!

January 22: Folk Music and Making Change

I was shocked last night to find that folk music is gone from SiriusXM radio. A petition to reinstate immediately sprung to mind. Sure enough, when I checked this morning about 700 had signed one and 1200 had liked the subject on Facebook. After major struggles with the CAPTCHA, (even the audio one which is hard to hear) I think I've signed it.

This has been the burning question for my generation: how to make change happen. From marching in the 1960s to occupying in 2011, this generation has done more than just vote. But it's hard to know what works. How many have to drop their subscriptions to make SiriusXM reconsider?

A friend of mine who is a business woman says letters count for more than e-mails. I'll write a letter to the CEO of SiriusXM and post it to my Facebook to see if any of my visitors will do likewise. I believe as Gandhi said, "You must be the change you want to see." I just hope it works.

January 23: Greedy for Knowledge

Is it greed? When the book awards that I started for children's books about disabilities were announced today, I immediately checked to see how many were available in accessible formats so I could read them. Two out of three are. Part of me wanted them all to be. I'm not greedy in the usual sense of wanting more than my fair share of money or things. But when it comes to knowledge or experiences, I may be greedy. In my defense, it's not usually a situation where if I get more, you get less.

When the wanting more is balanced by the joy in what I have, my conscience is clear. But when the drumbeat is more, more, more, I guess there's a problem.

The greed for knowledge comes from growing up with a very limited number of books available to me on record or in Braille. My town's public library was given a copy of the *World Book Encyclopedia* in Braille by a foundation. I think it was 150 volumes. I set out to read it all and got into the *C's* before realizing I couldn't remember everything. I became more selective and just read the entries that interested me.

Nowadays I have piles of magazines around that I can't bear to toss until I go through them for articles. I thought when I retired I'd get that done, but the piles grow and shrink episodically and still remain. I've checked with other retirees and the thought that you'll get through your piles (whatever they're of) in retirement is a myth. Maybe if I was greedy for the cleanest house, I'd do more pitching!

January 24: Good Conversations Instead of Tweets

My day started with a long phone chat with a friend I've known for over twenty years who lives in Iowa. We had lots of catching up to do since we hadn't chatted in a couple of months. Then we did some brainstorming on a project I'm working on. When I hung up I felt like we'd had a long visit at my dining table.

Luckily it was an unstructured day so the fact I got going an hour late didn't matter. That is one of the true joys of retirement to me—the good conversations I have time for. E-mails or tweets just aren't the same.

The only down side I can find in unstructured days is that I really find out which tasks on my "to do" list I want to do because they're the ones that get done and which I really don't care about doing. The garbage gets put out because it's a full can, but sorting through the magazines doesn't because it will keep.

I made time for friends when working, but it was rushed in ways it isn't now, especially with fellow retirees. Sometimes we can slow down to the speed of life.

January 25: Fixing Inaccessibility vs. Building It Right

Making it right is sure harder than building it right to begin with. This week the American Library Association Schneider family book award winners were announced. One of the winners was a graphic novel. It may be a fine book, but no blind person can read a graphic novel, no matter what kind of scanner or technology they have. A committee of librarians chooses the books, but since my name is on the award blind people have already complained to me about its being chosen. I've spent most of my free time this week getting over my hurt and then figuring out how to make it right and how to make it not happen again.

"Why would you do this?" I wanted to scream at the committee. When the local book festival heard this book had been chosen for this prestigious award, they wanted to bring the author to town on my nickel. I never typed a faster "no" than in the e-mail I sent back to them.

I strongly suspect neither the original committee nor the local book festival committee thought about what it would feel like to be asked to sponsor something that "your kind" of people can't have. Probably they've never had that experience of exclusion. The closest they've been is seeing *The Help* and thinking "it's awful to discriminate," but I never do it.

Three days after the announcement, I'm moving forward with how to come to terms with the choice, and how to prevent such a snafu in the future. Chopping ice on my front sidewalk has helped get there, as has talking to friends who "get it."

January 26: Savoring Poetry

When I was little I loved poetry and memorized quite a few poems. The rhyme and rhythm as well as the words resonated for me. It was like singing but you didn't have to be able to carry a tune, which I couldn't. Looking for "deeper meanings" in high school ruined poetry for me. It felt like shoving "man's search for meaning" down every poem's throat.

A few years ago I happened to read some Ted Kooser poetry because he'd been chosen United States poet laureate. I could understand it! His poem "The Leaky Faucet" which compared the water dripping to a voice calling "Cheer up . . . Someone will help you through your life," strikes me as brilliant.

Then I took a class at the library on Mary Oliver with a quintessential, gentle, wise English professor who never forced meaning down a poem's throat I'm sure. I love Oliver's imagery. In her poem "The Wild Geese" for example, "the world calls to you like the wild geese, harsh and exciting."

To sit and savor a poem is another luxury of retirement.

January 27: Young People

Next time I get on a tear about how rude and inconsiderate young people are these days, I must remember the two I talked to today. One, a recent college graduate who cleans houses for a living, is volunteering again to help me deliver pet food and supplies to elderly and disabled people next Saturday morning. Her truck, her time, and her gas are freely given because she loves animals and can't responsibly have one at this time.

Then there's the gal who is volunteering her music therapy skills to work with a very sick child I know. She's eking by with two small part-time jobs. I will give her gas money but may have to get pushy to make her take it.

Tomorrow when I work with my confirmation student on the sermon she has to write on John 15:17 "Love one another," I'll give her these examples of what love looks like.

January 28: Loving One Another on a Daily Basis

Today I worked with a confirmation student who had to write a sermon on John 15:17 "Love one another." I challenged her to look at an ordinary day and see the acts of love that made it happen. Her sermon challenged listeners to look at the little acts of love they either did or didn't do.

It was an exciting experience to work with a smart, sensitive, aware teen. She reminded me of me when I was that age and felt so keenly the shallowness and hypocrisy of people around me. At my age I still notice, but don't feel it as keenly and am more likely to turn the scope to ask, "am I responding lovingly to this shallow hypocrite? Am I being judgmental about people who judge?"

January 29: Being a Quart Low on Energy

Today I was a quart low on energy. It had been a tough, emotional week and I rose to the challenges, but suddenly I realized my tank was empty. I took my own oft-given advice. I talked to a friend, a long distance call, but I could feel the warmth and caring. Then I took a nap with a wonderful dog. When we got up I told her she needed to tell me I was wonderful. She managed to communicate "yes you are," and at the same time say "When's dinner?" I had a piece of chocolate for dessert, purely for medicinal purposes. I read a thriller, (nothing uplifting, but it got my mind off my world and into that cloak and dagger world.) Then I listened to a little relaxing music and prayed for a better tomorrow.

January 30: Pet Food Program People

By morning my energy tank was back up to normal and I chugged through a late January day, calling my customers for the WALOP program. The Eau Claire County Humane Association's We All Love Our Pets program provides food and supplies to elderly and disabled who have trouble getting out to purchase their own. Each person dotes on that animal in a unique way. Some seem to be very picky about what we bring them for free. After thinking about it, I've realized that they just want the best for that four-legged friend. Some will regale me with funny stories about their pet, such as the cat sleeping away the morning under the covers. Many have been on the program for over five years so they, their animals, and I have grown older. We have survived health issues, and chatted once or twice a month for long enough to become friends. We've had people and pets die, a marriage, an engagement, new pets, and friends of friends join the program. When pundits start to pontificate about people on welfare, I think of this group of people on social security or disability income. I hope the pundits know real people in tough situations like I do before they make rules. Friday we'll get the food from the Humane Association and buy what they don't have with local grant money. Then Saturday it's off to be a Litter Lady (as one of the program participants christened us) again. Fran loves to peek in the door and try to spot the cat so we both have fun.

January 31: Choices in Volunteer Work

Two very different kinds of volunteer work today represent the extremes of what's out there for retirees. Bagging rice in one-pound segments for the local food bank represents mindless work that is more fun because it's done with other volunteers. You meet new people, and can watch people, which is always fascinating. Is that young man interested in that young lady he's chatting up, or just doing it to pass the time? How will the group motivate that person who appears to be slacking? It's a lot to watch while trying to get exactly a pound scooped into a baggie!

Then I had a meeting with a doctoral candidate who has a disability and is in a mentoring study. Over lunch we shared bits of our lives very tentatively. Since we were assigned to each other, it feels like an arranged marriage. Will we like each other? Will my experiences from almost forty years ago of looking for my first professional job be of any use? This felt a lot more like work, except I'm not awarding a grade or pay as when I used to supervise young professionals. My advice comes free, take it or leave it, so it had better be good and not too frequent.

☽

February 1: Nudity Anyone?

I read the results of a fitness magazine survey today that said that two-thirds of people often walk around their houses naked. The article speculated that men were more likely to do this than women. I'm going to guess older people are less likely to do this than younger, unless you count people with dementia who don't remember to put clothes on. Even though we're having a January thaw here in Wisconsin, I'm also betting more people do this in warm weather and in warmer climes. Obviously lots of speculating on my part.

I like my body well enough, especially when it gets me where I'm going and is relatively pain-free. However, prancing around naked is not my style. It would be my luck that I'd walk in front of a window where someone had left the curtains open and I didn't know it. If the study is to be believed, there had better be two of you reading this that walk around naked to make up for me. Hope you're having fun!

February 2: Groundhogs

Headlines today give the forecast of the state's groundhog, but also debunk his forecasting ability. For over 125 years Puxatawny Phil and others have opined about how much winter is left. The defenders say the groundhog doesn't announce where there will be six more weeks of winter. The National Oceanic and Atmospheric Administration did a study that showed the groundhog's predictions didn't correlate with the length of the winter.

Why do we care? Because animals are cuter than politicians, and apparently they can be equally cantankerous. A groundhog took a nip out of Mayor Bloomberg, among others. It would be nice to know the future, even just the length of the winter, and groundhogs offer a prediction. And ultimately they are right, either there will be six more weeks of winter or there won't.

I'm not one of those modernists who want to replace a groundhog with a potbellied pig. Let the pigs predict the stock market.

February 3: Music Therapy for Non-Musicians

Today I helped start music therapy for a young gal I know with cancer. The therapist is a recent graduate from the university's now-ended music therapy program. Apparently in this fast-paced world it was decided there wouldn't be enough jobs in music therapy, and that the program was too labor-intensive for the university to support. But music is magical and we could even see it in the first session.

The parents, teacher, and I were all ready to sit back and watch, but it was clear if we didn't participate, the child wasn't going to either. Most of us were told sing quietly in music class, so it was hard. But by the time we got to the seventh verse of "The Cat Came Back" we were singing and shaking our rhythm devices with gusto, if not tune or rhythm. We probably reached our peak with "On Top of Spaghetti," an old camp favorite. We even rewrote the words to include Fran grabbing the meatball as it rolled toward the door. Even the music therapy student, young and serious about doing her very best, was laughing along.

Then she played short parts of popular songs to see what kinds of music the young child liked for future sessions. I found out that my devotion to classical and folk music put me three miles out from anyone else's tastes. I didn't even know what kind of music you'd call some of their selections.

The student happily signed up for future sessions. Goals may range from relaxation, improving movement, emotional expression, and other lofty ideas, but she was signing up for more fun with music. I can't wait to be invited back for a concert.

February 4: The Community of Pet Lovers

Today was pet food delivery day, and it was sunny and thirty-five degrees, quite a treat for February in Wisconsin. When I started this delivery program about six years ago, we had four customers—now we have about two dozen. I've never missed a month, although once I had to stretch it out to six weeks between deliveries because I was away getting a new dog. We've lost people who have had to move into a nursing home and a couple to death. It's such a community at work, from the Humane Association that sponsors it, to the volunteers who help me pick up and deliver the food, to the participants who invite friends to join it if they think the friend really needs it. And the animals, mainly cats who count on us to bring those huge boxes of kitty litter, so they can have a clean litter box and the food to keep them healthy and entertaining their owners. A couple owners have said their cat seems to know when we're coming and peeks around looking for Fran's nose to be poking around the door.

One gal knows a lot of the other recipients in her building, some members want to contribute, and a few are very picky about what we bring, just like in any other community. The volunteers often stay with the program for several years, save coupons, swap with each other so someone can have a vacation, and go with me to the hospital to visit an ailing owner. They care about the animals and know what those animals mean to their owners who are often poor, sick and not able to get out much. Community doing what a community should is fun to be part of even on a Saturday morning after staying out too late playing bridge the night before.

February 5: Sabbath

Trying to run today like a Sabbath, a day of rest is hard for me. My definition is no unnecessary work. So feeding the dog, cooking brunch for friends and cleaning up afterwards are okay, but working on projects would not be. I enjoy working on the Sunday National Public Radio puzzle, talking with friends, napping, and reading. But a part of me is restless; shouldn't I be doing more?

February 6: A Dash Day

Today is a "dash" kind of day. Linda Ellis's 1996 poem called "The Dash" talks about the time between your birth and death as "The Dash". Her point is even if you're not doing something major, it matters how you "live and love and how you spend your dash."

Nothing major happened today. I worked with a reader to read mail and pay bills. I answered e-mail and made phone calls to set appointments. Thinking about how I'm spending my dash enabled me to laugh about some misunderstandings on a project that I might have gotten mad about. I do notice in retirement that I can work harder on how I do the et cetera of life rather than just on the get it done part. It's too bad we can't find a way to spread this less stressed attitude to those who are still working. I wonder if Europeans who generally take more vacations than we do in the United States have more of this attitude.

February 7: Working Dogs

The United States Postal Service issued a block of four stamps (sixty-five centers) a couple weeks ago honoring a guide dog, a therapy dog, a search-and-rescue dog, and a military dog. I'm giving them as a valentine to a few people.

Today I went out to lunch with a friend to a pizza buffet to benefit our local soup kitchen. They seated us at a big table in front, right where people joined the buffet line. People from my church, book club, community organizations where I've spoken, and people who knew puppy raisers for Leader Dogs for The Blind here in town stopped by to chat. The first thing they saw as they came in was Fran's recumbent form lying mostly under the table. After a while, it became clear she knew she was the mayor of the town and people were stopping by to acknowledge that fact. She nobly accepted strangers' and friends' accolades and kept lying there. Afterwards, a friend dropped me off at the bank, I did my banking, and we trotted home. Her work as a guide dog is done well, but her work as an icebreaker is very important too. I think she knows that it's part of her job to reel people in so they'll talk to me. I guess she guides them to me just as she guides me safely.

February 8: Meetings by Phone

I went to a meeting by phone for two hours today.

Despite a bit of a sore ear, this is truly the way to go to a meeting. I had classical music on in the background, the perfect thing to listen to when I tired of listening to someone talk. I tried reading e-mail with one ear while listening to the meeting with the other ear, but I'm not that gifted in multitasking. The usual game of predicting who will talk next was available. There were long pauses between speakers while sighted people tried to predict when someone was done versus just taking a breath. I don't know what clues I use but I'm better at it. After all, all meetings are like phone meetings for me in that I don't get the visual clues anyway. Several people made comments about looking forward to the next meeting which is face-to-face, but not me! Looking interested is more work than I want to do in retirement.

February 9: Where is God?

A friend who has a dying family member asked me don't you wonder where God is in these situations? I've asked these types of question all my life about deaths, disabilities, poverty, job loss, etc.

It has gradually come to me that God is beside me, not absent, in the hard times. The question is where is God for me nowadays? More than, why did this happen?

I tried to tell her about my experience finding God in people who've reached out to me when I've been at my lowest. She said it doesn't happen that way for her. I wanted to encourage her to look for "God moments" as she mucked through this, but it seemed too much like preaching. She said that she wished she had my certainty and I said I wished she did too. I personally envy people who can comfortably witness to their faith, but I'm not there. I mumbled something about watching for angels-and not the kind who flap their wings-but I'll bet that's as clear as mud. Maybe a card, a pin, or some tangible reminder of my care is in order.

February 10: Little and Big "Imponderables"

Listening to BBC radio last night, I learned that they've figured out why zebras have stripes. Certain insects are less attracted to the stripes than they are to solid colors. Hearing the stripes explained made me think of the fun of reading David Feldman's columns and books about "imponderables" as he called them. Who hasn't wondered: *What Are Hyenas Laughing At, Are Lobsters Ambidextrous? How does Aspirin Find a Headache?,* or *Do Penguins Have Knees?* to name just a few of the imponderables he tackles.

Feldman writes well, combines a bit of science with a bit of wit, and in a page or less; he's answered the question definitively. I sure wish there were definitive answers to life's bigger questions, the why do bad things happen to good people kind of questions. Yes, there have been books written about them too, but even the answers found in religious scriptures have wiggle room in them. We live in that wiggle room and make it our own. Even though I yearn for a simple answer sometimes, when someone gives me one I don't trust it anyway. So we live the questions.

February 11: Heroes

With President's Day coming up, I've been thinking about heroes. I'll define a hero as someone who acts to make the world a better place. On my top twelve list are: Gandhi, Martin Luther King, Jr., Oprah, Louis Braille, Viktor Frankl, my first and fifth Seeing Eye dogs, Jesus, two priests I've known, and two former teachers.

A new list I want to make is of heroes for the aging journey.

Perhaps someone on the list should be Dr. William Thomas, a Harvard geriatrician who pioneered a new kind of elder housing. In these homes a dozen elders who needed skilled care could live and still be part of a home-like setting with self- determination of schedule.

Or maybe Doris "Granny D" Haddock, who walked across America starting at age eighty-nine to protest for campaign reform.
Or Sister Madonna Buder, who ran triathlons in her eighties.

Or Grandma Moses, who started painting in her seventies.

Or Benjamin Franklin, who helped write the Constitution when he was over eighty.

Or maybe the gal, who at age ninety-six got her last Seeing Eye dog. She inspires me when I think it's too nasty to go for a walk when it's below zero and I'm only in my sixties!

February 12: Wisdom of Donkeys

Today I spent a couple hours scanning *The Wisdom of Donkeys* so I could read it on a portable device. Several other "wisdom of" books ranging from *Wisdom of the Body* to *Wisdom of the Radish* were available in alternate formats, but not *The Wisdom of Donkeys.*

I think some of the wisdom is about slowing down and being patient, which is ironic because those are things I had to do to scan the book. I had to sit by the scanner and turn a page every thirty seconds, a totally mindless task. I can fall into "poor me" easily since I have to do two hours of work to read the book that sighted people don't have to do. However, I can also do "lucky me" because the scanner technology exists, and I own it, so I can read books that haven't been put into alternate formats.

I sat, scanned, and thought about and prayed for various friends. Now I can curl up and learn from donkeys.

February 13: Cosmetology Lecture

During the semester I give a lecture a week to classes ranging from kindergartners to graduate students about disability etiquette, how to serve customers with disabilities, and being a friend to a classmate with a disability. Today's request asks me to have more skin in the game than usual, or at least hair.

In ten days I'm going to a nearby community college to do a general talk and then spend an hour apiece in three different classrooms: architecture and design class, a human relations class, and a cosmetology class. Apparently the cosmetology class wants to cut my hair. It'll be good experience for them for when they have blind customers. They need to be able to communicate about hairstyles without resorting to pictures. My question is, will I need to keep the appointment I have made a week later with my regular beautician to clean up what they do?

Trusting a troupe of total strangers to understand what I want is a lot of trust for me. Too bad they're not vet tech students so they could trim Fran's nails or something less obvious. Friends I've talked to about it have offered suggestions such as, "tell them to feather it" and "well your hair grows fast doesn't it?" Of course I'll do it. When I was a student I got to counsel people, which is more important than a haircut. After this, teaching human relations skills to herd management, welding, and auto body students who are described by their instructor as "not talking much" should be a cinch.

February 14: Valentine's Day

According to Dr. Goodword, February 14 was originally a Roman feast day celebrating the beginning of the mating season of birds (hence the association with love). Chaucer was aware of this. In *Parliament of Foules* (1381), he wrote: "For this was on seynt Volantynys day Whan euery bryd comyth there to chese his make" (For this was on Saint Valentine's Day when every bird comes there to choose his mate). In the third century the celebratory day somehow became associated with a saint named Valentine. He was a priest and physician who was killed during the persecution of Christians by Claudius II. The connection between Valentine and the start of the bird mating season remains murky.

The possibilities of the love we could celebrate range from mating love, to priestly love and care for congregants, to love for friends to whom one sends a card. A story I received today from a puppy raiser for Leader Dog was the best love story I've heard in a long time. She had just met the young Marine her latest dog had been matched with. She and her family put a year of love and training into that pup and loved the idea of helping someone else enough to then say goodbye. Then trainers at the school worked with the dog for months to teach it its job. Finally, the young, blinded Marine ventured to the Leader Dog School and opened his heart to loving and trusting that dog.

Viva love! May everyone reading this be loved by someone special today.

February 15: Battle Fatigue

A LISTSERV thread I'm on had a topic about battle fatigue which struck a chord for me. Older blind people feel tired from all the access battles they've fought and lament, where is the next generation to fight the battles? I've heard this complaint in the women's movement too. I'm reading *Warmth of Other Suns,* a book about the

Black migration north, and hear the same tiredness from several of the main characters.

The LISTSERV is great for problem solving and resource sharing, but I don't find a lot of celebrating each other's victories. For me, when I'm tired of fighting, I need to consider filling my well in three ways: physically, emotionally and socially, and spiritually.

Physically: Am I not exercising, eating right, or getting enough rest because I'm consumed with fighting the good fight? Emotionally and Socially: Am I getting help for the fight, consolation for the setbacks, and celebration for the victories? Spiritually: Am I taking the time for prayer so that I'm centered in God's love and fighting for the right reasons in a Christian way?

Then there's the question that I need to ask myself often, am I playing enough?

It makes me want to break out in song. Perhaps joining Joan Baez in singing, "When you can't go on any longer, take the hand of a brother. Every victory brings another. Carry it on." Or Woody Guthrie's "This Land is Your Land."

February 16: An Average Day

I should have known it was going to be an odd day when Fran showed no interest in going to give a class talk. At first I thought it was the patchy ice on the sidewalks that was making her reluctant, but even when we got on campus she didn't want to go. About twenty percent of the big class apparently agreed and didn't show up. The rest of the class was quiet and uninvolved for the first twenty minutes but then got going and were full of questions. Fran was glad to come home and hang out. Even our game of bone was a mild one. I finished reading the book for next week's book club meeting, worked on a lecture for architecture design students about designing homes and public buildings to be blind-friendly, and even changed my e-mail password (after two calls to the help desk).

But the day remained just a day, nothing magical. It was sunny and temperatures hovered around thirty degrees. Maybe what Garrison Keillor says about Midwesterners needing really bad weather in the winter to feel good is true! I guess even in retirement, which is a wonderful time of life, some days are just average.

February 17: Strengths

I was working on a lesson about strength for a young friend who is dying of cancer. It made me notice many kinds of strength today. I went to a free foot care clinic and saw elders trundling in with walkers in hand, displaying physical strength, and smiles on their faces showing moral strength. I talked with the teacher of the student dying of cancer. . She has strong love and care for all her students and spent an hour after work on Friday thinking about what this student needs. I saw a strong sense of duty in Fran when she lay still while I had my toenails clipped instead of rolling around trying to get petted. I tasted strong flavors in the pad Thai I had for lunch, even though it was only a one on a four point scale of heat. I heard strong music as my favorite classical station played a Sibelius piece. I felt strong friendship coming from a cancer survivor's e-mail as she chattered about books and people we both know.

I realized strength is all around me if I have my antennae out for it.

February 18: Welcoming All of Us

My church missed an opportunity to be Christian and welcoming today. The Gospel was about a paralytic whose friends lowered him through the roof of a house on a mat and laid him at Jesus's feet to be healed. After Mass, people were invited downstairs (no elevator) to have a light supper for Mardi Gras. We don't have an elevator because of expense. However, it would have cost nothing for the priest to announce: "If you don't do stairs, please sit upstairs and one of us will come by and take your order." It could even be an assignment for confirmation students. They could be coached to not only bring up a plate for someone, but to sit and visit with that person. We have several church members who use walkers or wheelchairs. My guess is if they sat upstairs someone would eventually think to offer, do you need me to get you something? Nobody pushed it. After I cool off I'll e-mail the priest and suggest it for next year. I'm not ready to not be snarky yet. I wonder how long it will take.

February 19: Welcoming All of Us: Part Two

After regaling several friends with yesterday's story and hearing responses ranging from "that happens all the time" to "go get 'em!" I sent the priest the following e-mail:

The combination of yesterday's Gospel about the paralytic, a friend who uses a wheelchair nowadays sitting behind me, and our Mardi Gras party being downstairs hit me like a ton of bricks. Nothing was said about how those who don't do stairs could participate in the party. Next time we have that kind of party, would you be willing to add something like the following to your invite: "If you don't do stairs, please sit up here and somebody will be by to take your order and deliver some of that fine food to you." I'm sure that's how it would have played out if someone had stayed and asked for such help, but it is so much more welcoming to offer up front. What do you think?

The priest replied that in the past the church secretary had called people who might need this service and arranged it if they wanted it. I replied that announcing it in public alerted the community to help and would let them know that even if they didn't need it today it would be there if they did tomorrow.

February 20: Not Acting Old

How Not to Act Old by Pamela Satran grabbed my attention. It's cute and funny, but also sad to me. Satran tells us boomers not to e-mail (text, IM, and Facebook instead), to get rid of our poodle and get a cooler dog instead, and to stop saying "cool" and say "groovy", which is so old it's young again. She seems to think that the younger generation is so shallow that they don't want to hear about history, our health issues or much else that is not packaged in their lingo.

I'm sure sometimes this is true, but aren't people still caring individuals no matter what their age?

The last chapter suggests that we shouldn't die, or at least shouldn't acknowledge that we will. If we must die, cool ways, like accidents in exciting locales, are suggested and uncool ways, like being smothered by your blind cat in your own bed, are discouraged. I hope this book is at least partially tongue-in-cheek. I plan to occupy every day and every stage of my life, including dying, I hope.

If this book is trying to point out, as Sherwin Nolen said in *The Art of Aging*, we are the only animal that continues to develop during the later periods of our life and we should do this, then I wholeheartedly agree. To me it's a balancing act: learn new skills and lingo, but be proud of the wisdom you have gained. For this moment I'll define wisdom as knowing the consequences of actions. It's an expensive lesson, and I may be glad to share some, but I have a hunch that only a small part of this wisdom can be gained from others' experiences.

February 21: A Go-Go Day

Today was a go, go, go, twelve hour day with barely enough time between events to catch up on e-mail. I've got another one of those days this week and I am reminded of why I retired. All the events were good: talking to three classes of third graders, mentoring, voting, grocery shopping for the month, and a bit of snow shoveling for exercise. Tonight my legs and my brain are tired. I used to do this at least five days a week! I know the energy for each event suffered. Now I at least have the time to plan for the event and think about it afterwards.

February 22: Tea, Bars, and Lent

In the "if you build it they will come" mode yesterday I bought several containers of bars while doing my monthly grocery run. Today I had four visitors, each one stopped for tea, a bar, and conversation. Topics covered included a parent dying of cancer, learning's about sand mining gained by serving on the city/county health board, good books for a teen girl's birthday, and the ins and outs of Catholic rules for Lent.

Many years ago I decided that doing something positive during Lent rather than giving something up worked better for me. This year I'm going to spend at least five minutes a day in prayer. That means talking and listening for God's voice rather than just running my usual mental monologue. Today I jotted down a list of requests; God would have had to hurry to get them all down. Maybe forty days of this will help me slow it down a bit.

February 23: Simulating Aging

Massachusetts Institute of Technology has developed Agnes, a head-to-toe suit people can wear to simulate some of the physical changes that many elders experience. Glasses make fine print blurry. Bungee cords make arm extension difficult. Gloves make opening jars and door knobs challenging. Product designers can test whether their products are user-friendly for the elders they wish to market to.

Agnes sounds like a great idea. Of course, letting people live in the suit for a week or so would be even better! Now we need to figure out how to simulate brain farts, or whatever one calls them when a name just disappears, and being treated as old and unimportant. But to be fair, Agnes should also simulate the wisdom and wit of having lived many years.

Wouldn't it be fun to have an Agnes suit that you could whip out of your purse and hand to someone and just say "wear this for a while"?

February 24: Visible and Invisible work

Kahlil Gibran says that "work is love made visible." That's easy to acknowledge on a day when I'm giving four lectures like yesterday, but harder on a quiet day like today.

I answered e-mails, fed a friend tea and cookies, and cooked a meal for Friday night bridge. But there were also invisible pieces of work: prayers prayed, a dog played with, newspapers skimmed, and a nap taken to recharge batteries. I need to remember to be happy with both visible and invisible work.

February 25: Blooms in Winter

Even though it's been a mild winter, I'm tired of it. To make spring come faster, at least in my house, I'm forcing paper-white narcissus bulbs. They're just about ready to bloom and flood the living room with their magnificent scent.

They also make me think of the banner up at a church I used to go to that said "bloom where you're planted." There are two shining examples of this in my circle of friends and acquaintances. There's a friend of mine who lives in assisted living because of her physical disabilities. She's twenty years younger than the next youngest person living there. She buys large-print books and contributes them to the library. She does the same with puzzles and gives kid valentines to each fellow resident. Staff call on her to mentor new residents. She's blooming where others might sit and stew in anger at having to live there.

There's also one of the recipients of the pet food program I run. She lives in a high rise building for low-income seniors and people with disabilities. I call her the building's superintendent because she seems to know almost everyone and has a positive link with most. She shares the paper with someone, waters someone else's plants when they're gone, does Bible study with some, and calls to check on others. If there was a neighborhood watch, she'd be running it.

Both of these "bloomers" seem to take it for granted that you contribute wherever you can. The fact that they're blooming where they're planted makes it more spring-like, whatever the season.

February 26: Chocolate Rice Krispie Bars

It seems appropriate that on John Kellogg's birthday, a friend who wants to experience what it's like to do daily tasks as a blind person and I made rice krispie bars. She wore a blindfold so she couldn't peek. I'd bought chocolate rice krispie cereal which was on sale cheaper than the plain kind. My friend is a traditionalist and was deeply suspicious of them, but in the final analysis, we both declared them quite tasty. But when she took off her blindfold, she said "Oh they're brown. I wouldn't serve them to anyone." I sometimes forget that sighted people want it to look right as well as taste right. It reminds me of a beet and yogurt cold soup I took to a potluck. I swear I brought home as much as I took. Whether it was the fact it was pink soup, or because of the ingredients, I'm not sure. It's easy for me to say, but if someone serves you something that looks odd, close your eyes and at least give it a try!

February 27: Occupy Our Food Supply Day

February 27 marks "Occupy our Food Supply Day". It's a day of global action to unite the Occupy movement with sustainable farming, food justice, buy local, slow food, and environmental movements.

Take back *your* food supply by supporting a local food or co-op, by purchasing directly from local farmers, or by planting a garden. When you spend money in your community, you support a healthy local economy. With every seed you plant, you take a small step towards ecological and personal health.

Since I shop once a month and need to get everything I need from one store, I can't do the co-op shopping. That leaves slow food and gardening. Voles or some other kind of garden pests devastated my tomatoes last year. If I was relying on gardening I'd be awfully hungry.

What can I do about slow food, at least today? I thought I knew what it meant until I found a cookbook for *Slow Food Fast*. I thought it meant cooking from scratch. It turns out it means good, clean, and fair food, combining the pleasure of food with a commitment to community and environment. Just to play it safe, since I don't have a clue about the conditions my grocery store food was grown in, I'll eat something out of a jar canned by a friend. I know the care she and her husband take in their growing from their own seeds and putting up most of their own food. Thank goodness they're community-minded and share with lazy people like me.

February 28: Being Productive When Sick

Today was my day to be sick with an upper respiratory thing. I barely got my jobs for the day done. Otherwise it was nap, take the dog out, eat, nap, and take the dog out again. Luckily, she is a great napper, so we agreed several naps were just fine. She also fancies herself to be quite the diagnostician—making her assessments by smelling my face and my behind. As I've begun to re-enter the human race, she's upping her requests for playtime. I sure don't like being unproductive. This needs to change or at least I need to change, my definition of productivity to include praying, reading, and listening to music.

February 29: Leaping

For the five million Leapers on the planet, today is a special day. They get to celebrate their birthdays on the actual day, not the day before or the day after. Members of this elite club have included Rossini, George M. Cohan, Jimmy Dorsey and Dinah Shore. Not only are Leapers 1cheated out of cake and presents, but some monumental bureaucratic nightmares have occurred.

But for most of us, it's just an extra day. If we're female, we can propose instead of waiting for the question to be popped, according to tradition.

This year we were digging out from a big snowstorm. Students in grade and high school got the day off. I chose to use my extra day to finish reading my March book club selection. Unfortunately, two golden retrievers died in it, so my half golden retriever had to comfort me as I sniveled into her fur.

Now there are many more "productive" things I could have done, but somehow today it was okay that I lie around and read. It's an extra day!

☽

March 1: Teaching Manners

I was grousing to a friend about the lack of manners in a twenty-something today. The friend gave me two new perspectives about why I should educate the miscreant. The ungrateful graduate student had not thanked me for filling out a survey for her thesis study, which took me at least a half hour to do. I was up on my soapbox that a one line e-mail was not too much to expect, but had not been forthcoming.

"Do I have to teach her?" I whined. My friend said yes because we are the elders and it's our job to instill the mores of society. She also pointed out that in a wolf pack the older wolves would definitely nip the younger ones into correct behavior.

March 2: Dr. Seuss's Birthday

Today is Theodore Geisel's birthday—perhaps you know him as Dr. Seuss. In case you don't have a grandchild or kid friend close enough to read to, you might enjoy celebrating the day by reading his book for "obsolete children" *You're Only Old Once!*

It takes you through a visit to the Golden Years Clinic. From the initial solvency test to diagnostics, treatment, and medicating; it's all there. You'd swear Dr. Seuss was at your last run-in with the medicos.

Unfortunately, this is the only book he wrote with the aged in mind. If you're feeling creative, take on other common aging issues like applying for social security, trying to buy a piece of modern electronics that you can actually figure out how to work or getting customer service that actually helps.

If all that wears you out, just curl up with *The Cat in the Hat* or your favorite Seuss book, milk and cookies, and a blanket and celebrate "Read Across America" day in his honor.

March 3: Spotting Goodness

As I was gearing up to deliver pet food, I read a "Thought for the Day" online about spotting goodness. I decided to take the challenge today and see how much goodness I could spot.

Some of my finds included:

The twenty-something volunteer who showed up on time and cheerful to load her truck with the thirteen boxes of kitty litter and pet food, plus Fran and me to go do our deliveries;

The shoveling jobs most recipients had gotten done so we only had to slither up and down a few un-shoveled walks;

The thanks and the loving comments most recipients made about their critters;

The goodness of leftovers so I didn't have to cook today;

The joy of a nap;

The lovely visit of a friend;

A helpful stranger at Mass who lent me his arm in the communion line;

And the wonders of having a stack of fine books to curl up with to say nothing of a fine dog at the end of a great day.

I may take this challenge again soon. It was fun.

March 4: Playing all Day

Today I played all day. I'll rest tomorrow.

Fran and I cooked and entertained for brunch. A friend read the best newspaper cartoons of the week to me. I played Scrabble with a human, and chase with Fran, took a walk, went out for ice cream, visited friends, talked on the phone, and went to bed exhausted and smiling. "All work and no play makes Jack a dull boy," as I heard growing up. Today was decidedly not a dull day.

Play, from golf to bridge, is recommended to seniors to keep our minds sharp and keep us in social contact. It probably helps the economy too! I kicked it up a level by downloading a new computer game of audible tennis called "Crazy Tennis." So far my score is zero but maybe I'll figure it out next game. At least when you start with a score of zero, you can only go up. Reading instructions netted me a score of

84; using earphones to get directional sound got me 346 the first try. Can Wimbledon be far off?

Part of the fun to me is watching how others play. My Scrabble play is highly competitive. Fran plays a different game of tug-of-war with each human. She must enjoy seeing how others play too.

March 5: Having Hard Conversations

Today I had a couple of hard conversations. I squirmed around before having them, whining to myself that I was retired and shouldn't have to work. The people in question should know the right thing and do it. It finally occurred to me that unless I was retiring to life as a hermit on an island, I couldn't retire from human interactions.

When I finally said what I needed to, phrased in proper assertive wording, "I feel…," "Because my experience tells me…,"and "I want you to…," I got good responses in both situations. Of course, just because I'm properly assertive and not aggressive doesn't guarantee a good response, but this time I got lucky.

The only hard part was to get off my tail and do it. Queen Margaret II of Denmark once said that she had a dream of becoming "a passenger in my life." Sometimes being a passenger would be easier, but I might not like where it would go. So I acted and then I celebrated by playing more Crazy Tennis, top score 464.

March 6: Three Foods

This is a foodie discussion, but not the typical eat the Mediterranean diet, keep calories low, and add anti-aging foods from avocados to yogurt to your diet discussion. I'm convinced all that is good advice, but today is a celebration of a couple foods purely because of their taste.

Consider the question: if you could only have three foods, what would they be? Here are my nominations:
Chocolate, today Oreos:

One hundred years ago today, tins of Oreos were sold for $0.30 per pound. Five hundred billion cookies later, they're still the world's favorite cookie. My personal favorite is the chocolate-covered Oreo with mint filling.

Beans: Adding black beans to chili, garbanzos to spaghetti, and a little French dressing on cooked lentils makes a great spread. I know some are peas not beans and they're mixed with things, so it's not really a fair choice. The added fiber, protein, and taste are worth trying.

Cheese: Of course in Wisconsin we deep fry cheese curds for a snack, taking our cheese to a new level. I also encountered *gjetost* (Norwegian goat cheese) for the first time in Wisconsin. Any way you spread it, cheese rules. With fruit it might even make an acceptable alternative to Oreos, if you've given up chocolate for Lent.

March 7: Young People and Technology
I wanted to read *Fault in Our Stars,* a book about a teen with cancer. The library system had it on MP3 CD. It is one CD instead of many because it's MP3 format. My old CD player doesn't do that format. So I called the library to see if it's legal to download it onto an MP3 device (my book port). They didn't know if it was legal and didn't know if it was even technically possible. They said, "Well, nobody will come after you." So I did it and it works. It cheers me to find people younger than me who don't know any more than I do about technology. It's an excellent young adult novel, and a good reminder to all of us to notice life as it happens.

March 8: International Women's Day
It's International Women's Day which makes me want to celebrate the many strong women I have known and learned from. There's my mom who gave me a love of reading and a strong sense of doing the right thing, several teachers taught kindness by example as well as their subjects, and women friends have walked beside me through tough times.
All of these women were wonderful human beings, and strong women. Over two thousand years ago Proverbs 31 described some of the virtues of a good woman and they're still to be emulated today. They include: working with willing hands, taking care of home and hearth as well as business, and caring for the poor. "Strength and dignity are her clothing, and wisdom and kindness come out of her mouth." Proverbs 31:25. Even back then, women got to do it all, working inside and outside the home. Equal pay and equal rights weren't stipulated then and haven't been achieved yet. A strong woman gets to fight for justice too.

I wonder why this day isn't celebrated as much as Mother's Day is, at least not in the United States.

Will you celebrate by being inspired with quotations from *The Words of Extraordinary Women*, be helped by the current edition of *The Female Stress Syndrome*, or be amused by one of Haywood Smith's *Red Hat Club* novels?

March 9: Books about Living Forever

Another way you can tell boomers and beyond are occupying aging is that there's starting to be a definite tilt on the self-help/advice best seller lists toward living forever and never getting old books. Take the current two entrants in this booming field: *An End to Illness* by Agus and *Use Your Brain to Change Your Age* by Amen.

They contain good advice, like being your own doctor; knowing your risk factors so you can individualize your health improvement plan, getting plenty of social support, reducing stress, consuming less sugar and trans fats, increasing exercise, and eating organic foods. It's all good advice, authoritatively and wittily delivered, but the titles are over advertising. Why should we need to be promised something that doesn't exist to get us to buy, read, and possibly implement the good advice between the covers of these books? Yes *an End to Illness* is sexier than *Reducing Your Illness Risks* but it isn't true. Also such titles imply to me that those who are ill and/or aging are responsible for the bad outcomes they may be experiencing, so lose our sympathy, empathy, and care. When there are more and more of us boomers and beyond and medical costs skyrocket, I could see rationing based on behavior. Are you overweight? Shame on you; you don't get that new knee. Maybe I'm paranoid; time will tell.

March 10: Empty Bowls Fundraiser

One of my favorite volunteer gigs each year is taking tickets at the Empty Bowls fundraiser for Feed My People, a food bank distribution service for several Western Wisconsin counties. It's a good cause and well-supported by everyone, from young families to senior citizens. They serve soup at lunch and supper as well as selling pottery and wooden bowls crafted by school, college, and local crafters. When I take people's tickets, I usually ask to feel the bowls they've chosen. There were bowls shaped like elephants and cats; beautiful sleek bowls made of cherry wood and even a bowl a minister planned to use as a wine chalice. One joker put my hand on his rather round stomach when I asked to see his pot! After that I started using the word bowl more.

About 1400 people came to the event and over $40,000 was raised. Admiring art, seeing friends, eating wonderful potato leek soup, and helping a good cause — what a way to spend three hours.

March 11: Applying for a Purpose Prize

Today I applied for a Purpose Prize for a project undertaken in the second half of life. I want my children's book *Your Treasure Hunt: Disabilities and Finding Your Gold* to be in every library in the country and in every pediatrician's hands. It's a springboard for parents, teachers, or medical professionals to use to talk with kids about the hard parts of having a disability, but also to help the child build self-esteem and find the treasures in their life. I self-published it two years ago, and have sold almost one thousand copies, mainly by word of mouth. It did win a Moonbeam award and will be published in print/Braille by the National Library Service for the Blind.

Because I self-published it and had to hire a graphic designer to illustrate it, I'm still in the hole on this project. At this point it's like I took a quite expensive vacation to Europe. It was something I had to do because there is no similar book, and I want kids with and without disabilities to understand what it's like. Putting up big bucks to publish the book is one of the biggest investments I've made. It sort of felt like the first time I bought a house, exciting, scary, but clearly a piece of my calling to leave the world a better place.

I doubt the prize will come to me, but that's not the point. It's good that some new ventures taken on by people in their second half of life will be celebrated. I celebrate what I did by writing about it.

March 12: Girl Scouts

Were you a Girl Scout? I was, as were three million women. Today is girl scouting's one hundredth birthday. Selling cookies to a buyer who opened their box and offered me one and lashing a latrine cover out of sticks were two of my biggest memories from scouting days. Maybe selling cookies trained me for the fundraising I do from time to time for various volunteer organizations. I'm not sure what the learning to lash sticks together did for me.

Nowadays I'm a Red Hat, which in some ways reminds me of Girl Scouts. It's a group for fun and friendship for women over fifty. My group has wonderful cooks (our potlucks are to die for) and good natured women who laugh a lot at our meetings. Tomorrow night we'll have fondue and play some game involving dice and dimes. What we do doesn't matter so much; it's the banter and the warmth of friendship that sticks with me. Social support (as the pundits call it) rocks!

March 13 Getting and Giving:

It's another day of filling my bucket with social support. A book club, a talk in a third grade class, and a Red Hat party occupied the day. The weather was warm for March and people were all loving and kind toward each other. I don't know if everybody was in such a good mood because of the beautiful weather, but it was a lovely day. The comment of one young man in the third grade class was typical for the day. After I'd given my talk, we had a petting line where students could meet Fran. After she'd licked him, he said, "I'm never going to wash off where she licked me." I hope I can remember this day when the weather and people's moods are cloudier.

March 14: Taking a Ceramics Class (Preparation)

I signed up for ceramics in June through Continuing Education. I've already e-mailed with the prof about accommodations and she sounds wonderful. She's taught blind students and was willing to do my glazing or have me bring a sighted friend to do it. Fran and I will be college women!

I'll have to get someone to teach me my way to the classroom. I sure hope the other students are friendly and maybe even helpful. I'll have to move around in the studio without being guided by Fran when I need to wash my hands and dump my water bucket. I've downloaded a book on pottery; that's always my solution to the unknown, read ahead and gather as much information as I can.

March 15: Friend's Goal of Becoming a Guardian Angel

I was talking to a lady I know today who passed eighty several years ago. Just last week she decided to go on hospice service. Family members are with her and she's in no pain. She says she's ready to go and wants to be someone's guardian angel when she gets to heaven.

I'm sure she will be because that's what she's done on earth— raise her children, cook and bake for all she knew, and quilt for church service projects. She'll be a really hard working angel. Whoever gets her for a guardian angel will be lucky.

Funerals nowadays are celebrations of life and I'm sure hers will be. It will be the duty for those of us who knew her to minister to her family, who will be bereft, I'm sure.

I hope those who don't have a strong faith like this lady have something to help their passing be as easy. Yesterday I went to hear a talk by the Threshold Singers, who try to do that for people who are dying or crossing other important thresholds. Their songs emphasize peace, love, and breathing in strength. New Age spirituality isn't my thing, but it provides something for those for whom Christianity isn't their thing.

As for me, when my time comes, please have old hymns (but not "Amazing Grace" playing or sung by a barbershop quartet with a jig or two thrown in.

March 16: Wabi Sabi

Today's e-mail included a column by Sr. Joyce Rupp about the Japanese concept of *wabi sabi*. It puts into words something I believe strongly but have never been able to articulate, that the flaws in something are valuable too.
It acknowledges the realities that nothing lasts, nothing is perfect, and nothing is finished.

This concept of flawed beauty, as opposed to beauty from perfection, seems to me to apply to humans and animals as well. For example, my current Seeing Eye dog has scratches on her nose from a scrap she got into with a sibling when she was a pup. One of the trainers kind of apologized for it. To me, it shows a beautiful part of her character, which is she sometimes sticks her nose where it doesn't belong. I admit I think that's beautiful because it's like me!

I wonder as we age if we become more able to see *wabi sabi* beauty. I also wonder if there's any way we can help the young catch hold of this concept and quit pressuring themselves and others for unattainable perfection. When I was a counseling psychologist on a college campus, a lot of the counseling I did with students was on this theme.

Too bad I didn't have the name of the concept to give my ideas a name. I guess my counseling was *wabi sabi* too.

March 17: Irish

I don't have any Irish in me, but today I wish I was. The sly humor, the blarney, the jigs and reels, the heart put into things, the poetry, and storytelling make me wish I had Irish blood. I know the Irish saved civilization when my Germanic forebears were mainly engaged in tribal fighting.

I guess I'll have to settle for reading a Maeve Binchy novel, eating potatoes and cabbage (I'm a vegetarian so no corned beef), and listening to Irish music all day. Then I'll go to Mass and meditate on this Yeats quote: "Being Irish, he had an abiding sense of tragedy which sustained him through occasional bouts of joy."

March 18: Growing Up, Kicking and Screaming

You're never too old to grow up.-—Shirley Conran

When this quote popped into my mailbox today, I knew it was meant for me! Yesterday I'd been through a doubleheader of difficult situations and had only whined a little. Maybe I'm growing up a little?

One of the Scripture readings we often have during Lent is Chapter 9 of John about the man born blind. Jesus cures him but the Pharisees try to pick a fight about it with him and his parents. The Pharisees point out it was done on the Sabbath, which was a no-no. The sermon preached this day was better than many I've heard. The priest talked about how when Jesus comes to us we often don't understand quickly who He is. It avoided all the usual clichés about amazing and/or pitiable blind people. Unfortunately, it was followed by the hymn "Amazing Grace." It's a beautiful hymn and people love to sing it, but the line "was blind but now I see" gives me the willies. I know it's a metaphor for I didn't understand but now I do, but it makes me cringe because of how it equates blindness with not understanding.

The second half of the evening was spent being a Public Radio Association rep at a local concert co-sponsored by Wisconsin Public Radio. I went with a sighted friend who was asked if I needed an elevator, wanted a chair, needed a name tag, or wanted some food. Apparently the people who spoke to my friend instead of me have picked up the idea that if you can't see, you can't understand. Of course I politely answered the questions directed to my friend about me. Maybe it will be different next time. I walked away thinking, "So many people to educate, and so little time." I am saddened by the unintentional exclusion at a musical event where blindness shouldn't be a problem.

The growing up part is that after this double-header, I'm not in orbit with righteous anger, just a bit sad. The birds are still singing and I'm still listening.

March 19: Hospitality

Today is the feast day of St. Joseph. I'm told that some Italians celebrate by inviting people over for a meal, a St. Joseph's table. Being one who will celebrate at the drop of a hat, I dedicated the day to being hospitable in the spirit of a St. Joseph's Day table. Two people came for meals, tea, and talk. I also focused on hospitality by really listening to them. Sometimes it was hard to listen, like when the vet told me about a possible problem in my guide dog's annual physical. I wanted to argue. It was hard to listen with an open heart when someone was prattling on about something I didn't care about.

In retirement I have more time to explore hospitality. I'm finding out it is hard work to truly be hospitable.

March 20: Spring

Happy spring! I just love the bird songs, the smell of hyacinths and lilacs, the taste of fresh asparagus, and the feel of the warm sun of spring. I can even celebrate a warm spring rain, especially if I'm on the inside listening to it on the roof and don't have to go anywhere.

Spring is a time of new beginnings—time to spring into a new project. The one that is percolating for me is a Disability Welcome Wagon. As we age, more and more people who've never had a disability develop one or more of them. There are a myriad of governmental and nonprofit groups serving people with any given disability. People may need adaptive equipment, but may not know that there is a gizmo for their particular need and if so, where to get it. Then there are tricks of the trade that people with a disability develop to deal with a particular problem. This welcome to Disabilities Wagon Team, I'm imagining, would consist of volunteers who have intimate knowledge of particular disabilities and who would make contact with newcomers to their disability group upon request. They'd know the maze of agencies, non-profits, self-help groups, and help people plug in to them. More importantly, they'd be living proof that a good life is there to be had with that disability.

For a more contemplative introduction to spring, read Mary Oliver's poem "Spring" or consider Robert Frost's words: "Oh, give us pleasure in the flowers today; / And give us not to think so far away / As the uncertain harvest; keep us here / All simply in the springing of the year."

March 21: Bach's Birthday

Today is J. S. Bach's birthday. If I was on a desert island with the music of only one composer to listen to, it would either be Bach or Beethoven. Bach's style, particularly his counterpoint, is so intellectually stimulating. I love hearing his works played on piano, organ, or even guitar. How anyone could write a fugue in every key is a mystery to me. When I was taking piano lessons, I learned a few simple Bach pieces and I loved them. They seemed almost mathematical to me in their precision. Three hundred years after his death, he's still popular such that Madison, among other cities, has a "Bach Around the Clock" public performance to celebrate his birthday.

Happy birthday, J. S. Bach. I think I'll kick back, listen to Bach, and maybe have a bock beer to celebrate.

March 22: James Patterson

It's the birthday of the world's best-selling novelist, who has written over seventy novels. He's not that many years old! His secret of success, he says, is to tell stories the way ordinary people do, leaving out the parts people would skim over. I can't imagine writing that much. I'll just have to pick up James Patterson's latest and start it today to see if the murderer is caught.

It'll be quite a contrast to the other book I'm reading, Molly Peacock's *Paper Garden* a biography about an eighteenth century gentle lady who did her major creative work after age seventy, mixed-media collages of flowers. The writing is poetic, personal, and lushly descriptive.

What a joy it is in retirement to have time to read all kinds of books for pleasure.

March 23: Being Part of a Community

Being part of the community means a lot to me. Today was a good community day. I got to share my knowledge of assistive technology with a stroke survivor who needed a talking computer. I showed him several devices and told him my two rules for learning to use assistive tech devices:

1. They aren't perfect or as good as what you had before disability, but they are better than nothing.
2. There's a steep learning curve. You'll hate it for six weeks to six months, but hang in there.

Often people are given a piece of adaptive equipment and assume it'll be wonderful and solve all problems right out of the box. Then when it doesn't, they get frustrated, feel stupid and overwhelmed, and put it on the shelf. What a waste! I hope by warning this man up front of the steep learning curve and offering to help him learn to use his equipment successfully.

I went to a fish boil, a Lenten fundraiser for a local Catholic church. I needed help through the cafeteria line and the gal who helped me knew me from a meeting long ago.

Overall, it was a good day where I got to help and be helped by my community.

March 24: Fannie Crosby

Fannie Crosby a blind poet and prolific writer of hymns would be 192 today. She said of her blindness that, "if I had a choice, I would still choose to remain blind ... for when I die; the first face I will ever see will be the face of my blessed Savior."

Blind for all of her life, Fanny Crosby, the greatest hymn writer in the history of the Christian Church, later wrote, "And I shall see Him face to face, and tell the story - Saved by grace." She put over eight thousand poems to music, and over one-hundred million copies of her songs were printed. As many as two hundred different pen names, including Grace J. Frances, were given her works by hymn book publishers so the public wouldn't know she wrote so large a number of them. She produced as many as seven hymn-poems in one day. On several occasions, upon hearing an unfamiliar hymn sung, she would inquire about the author, and find it to be one of her own!

Fanny gave the Christian world such songs as: "A Shelter In The Time Of Storm," "All The Way My Savior Leads Me," "Blessed Assurance," "He Hideth My Soul," "Pass Me Not," "Praise Him Praise Him," "Rescue The Perishing," "Tell Me The Story Of Jesus," and "To God Be The Glory".

To me the comfort of a good hymn like "He Hideth My Soul" is more than the sum of a sing-able tune and true words. It speaks to a deep longing in my soul and gets into those deep places where comfort is needed like water sinks into parched earth.

As long as I'm on the subject of hymns I like, here's another. When they have my funeral, they could use a couple of Crosby's hymns and then this one, but if they use "Amazing Grace" I'll haunt them!

We Walk by Faith
Text: Henry Alford, 1810-1871
Music: Attr to Hugh Wilson, 1766-1824

We walk by faith, and not by sight;
No gracious words we hear
of him who spoke as none e'er spoke,
but we believe him near.

We may not touch his hands and side,
nor follow where he trod;
yet in his promise we rejoice,
and cry, "My Lord and God!"

Help then, O Lord, our unbelief,
and may our faith abound;
to call on you when you are near,
and seek where you are found:

That when our life of faith is done
in realms of clearer light
We may behold you as you are
in full and endless sight.

March 25: In love with life

An encouragement e-mail asked: are you in love with life? "Of course I am," I quickly replied in my mind. But as I thought about it, I reflected that the way I love life has changed over the years. There are still the awestruck moments, but mostly it's the comfortable, companionable kind of love that I have with old friends. As friends pass away, it reminds me that my time will also come, and the intense enjoyment of life's little pleasures increases for a while. Small things like the bird song, the ice cream cone, the warmth of the sun, are more beautiful.

How do I tell life I love it? I'll share the splashes of joy with others, say yes to noticing them, and look for more.

March 26: Give Me Patience, Now!

One of my character flaws is lack of patience. Goodness knows I need it! John Milton (who was blind) said in his Sonnet on Blindness that "he serves who only stands and waits". There's a lot of waiting in disabled peoples' lives and I don't do it well. Today I decided to work on patience in two ways: I left word for a call back for a second time with an institution, and I prepared to read a book on patience. Since the book wasn't available in alternate formats, I had to spend about an hour and a half scanning the pages one-by–one, waiting to copy the book, so my talking computer could read them out loud later. Now I'm grateful I can eventually read the book, and I'm grateful the institution's representative did call me back eventually, but those aren't the most important parts.

I monitored my impatient thoughts and found the most frequent ones to be: I'd rather be doing something else, that person should call, and life should be easier. Playing the game of, what good can I think about, helped a little. So did re-labeling the waiting as character building. The fact that I was waiting for a phone call while I did the scanning also helped; at least I was waiting in two directions at the same time.

After reading, or at least impatiently skimming two books on patience, I'm pondering these points:

Patience would actually help me save time by not wasting it fretting.

Take the, I'm still learning, this too will pass perspective.

I have all the time I need.
Some things are worth waiting for.
It will take as long as it takes.
What am I reacting to in this person and why?
Impatience is just another form of perfectionism.
It takes patience to develop patience!

March 27 TED Talks

Today I went to a TED talk on music, the brain and music therapy. TED talks are videos of people talking about a "big idea worth talking about." After the video a local expert talked. This one was held on campus and although many students were there was a good sprinkling of community members including several retirees.

Being able to hear a lecture on a topic of interest is a great use of technology. Many universities are now putting some classes on the Internet for free download. There are so many opportunities to learn.

After looking over that talks available at ted.com, I'm also thinking I want to teach. There's very little on disability issues. Talks on aging are primarily about, preventing premature aging, what are you going to do with your aging parents, type without much on the positives of aging. I'll have to stir up some discussions.

March 28: Living with a new disability

A consultation today with an elder going blind has made me expand my rules for assistive technology into six rules for living with a new disability:

1. It costs more, takes longer, and requires more planning to live with your new disability.
2. There's a huge learning curve. You are a baby in this new life, so don't expect the same results when you do a familiar task.
3. Gizmos, adaptive tech gadgets, etc. are great, but will not "fix" your disability.
4. Some people, be they friends, family, or professionals, will "get it" and be helpful; some you can coach into responding well and some you can't.
5. There are positives of having the disability, but it will take a while to find the pearls. Remember, it takes a grain of

sand irritating an oyster plus a lot of calcium carbonate secretion for an oyster to make a pearl.

6.   Go ahead and feel good and sorry for yourself. Throw a pity party. Then when you get tired of it, get up and move on.

March 29: Myths about Aging

In *A Long Bright Future*, the author lists five myths about aging: old people are sad and lonely, your whole fate is foretold in your genes, retire out of the work force as soon as you can, old people are a drain on the world's resources and how we fare in old age is an individual matter, not societal.

In fact, mental health generally improves with age, aside from dementias. Older people are on average happier, perhaps because we savor what we have, knowing time is flying. The author points out that there is a divide between the kind of life enjoyed by the wealthy and healthy aged, and the poor and disabled aging. The poor die younger by almost five years and this difference is increasing. Income predicts how quickly health declines and education predicts health status even with chronic health conditions.

Good ideas for those of us who are already aging include designing our environments to support healthy lifestyle choices, and supporting policies that provide health care for people at all income levels. We should diversify social supports, and activities as well as investments. Keep learning and contributing. Keep moving and consider getting a dog. I liked the fact that this book appealed to us, the aged, to support political policies that will ensure quality of life to future generations instead of just saying we want ours. Maybe I will go back on the Aging and Disability Resource Center board as my small contribution to making institutions better.

March 30: Eating and dining

I believe the actor Maurice Chevalier got it right when he said "I never eat when I can dine." I love to nurture friends with home cooked meals. I could write at least an addendum to *Heartbreak Recovery Kitchen* about my experiences contributing to people's healing with a meal and/or a cup of coffee and conversation.

One of many reasons I love the Internet is the variety of recipes that are available. I knew I wanted to use cabbage and potatoes in a dish for company. A Google search turned up scores of possibilities ranging from an Ethiopian dish to an Irish dish. Finally I settled on col cannon, the Irish dish. It promises to be ready in thirty minutes.

It was easy to fix and very good. Once again simple home cooking produced a fine inexpensive meal. All diners left with smiles on their faces.

March 31: Greatest Songs Ever

Rolling Stone magazine offered a list of greatest songs ever, starting with "Rolling Stone" by Bob Dylan. Obviously favorites depend on your musical tastes, and mood at the time. It's fun to consider if you could only have ten on your player, what would they be? Today, in no particular order, here are mine:
"Clouds" or "Both Sides Now",
"Ode to Joy"
"You'll Never Walk Alone"
"Climb Every Mountain"
"Be Not Afraid"
"Christ the Lord Has Risen Today"
"Hard Times Come Again No More"
"You Raise Me Up"
"We Shall Overcome"
"To every Thing There Is a Season"

I guess I look for hope in hard times from my songs.

April 1: April Fool's Day

Today is one of my favorite holidays because it's not commercialized and everyone can enjoy it no matter what religion, ethnicity, or age they are. This year I caught three out of four people with my offering. After solicitously asking if they'd made their grocery run and getting back "No. Why?" I told them there was going to be a foot of snow tomorrow. It was 45 and sunny at the time. Only one person said "Yeah right, on April 2." The others just groaned when I said "April Fool's"

One of my best jokes was a notice in all the mailboxes of my undergraduate dorm announcing that next year all rooms would be co-ed. This was in 1967 and it did fool several students. Of course most didn't read "official" notices anyway and just tossed it.

The best joke I heard this year was of phone lines set up by a zoo. You could call your friends and tell them to call "Anna Conda" or "Don Key" or "Mr. Wolf" at xxx-xxx-xxxx. Better block your number before doing this if your friends have caller ID. If the hapless victim does call they hear the animal's sound followed by a human announcing that they've been pranked and suggesting they sponsor that animal on the zoo's Friends website.

Isn't human ingenuity wonderful!

April 2: Reading in Retirement

In retirement I've let myself slack off in reading self-help and psychology books, opting instead to increase fiction reading. Early this morning I finished a Clive Cussler thriller. Mysteries and thrillers that are good enough to stay up late to finish are one of the joys of being retired. To me they need to have at least one likable character, not too much graphic violence, an interesting setting, some scientific info or good trade craft descriptions, and enough action to keep me awake when listening to it lying in bed. Some of my favorite authors include: Baldacci, Clancy, Preston and Child, Patterson, Palmer, Berry, Steinhauer, Rankin, Mills, Lescroart, Kava, Penny, Griffin Martini, Rimington, and for a police procedural Michael Connely. By the time I add a few memoirs, books on aging and disability issues, and anything by Maeve Binchy, I'm falling behind. I do like to keep up with serious children's books like *The Book Thief, The Absolutely True Diary of a Part-time Indian,* and the *Fault in our Stars.* I'll have to try *Hunger Games* because it's such a sensation. I do want to know what my niece is talking about.

April 3: Take a Poem to Lunch

I was reading about ways to celebrate poetry month, and one of them appealed to me, take a poem to lunch. I went to www.poets.org and chose a Viorst poem about "Mother Doesn't Want a Dog." The punch line after describing the negatives of dogs involves, but she's really not going to want this snake.

Most people were wary of having a poem at the table with them, but enjoyed it immensely when it was read. Some came up with memories of mothers who enjoyed poetry. The children and tweens I shared it with laughed and readily shared poems they liked, or found one on the Internet to share. Adults unfortunately also had memories of not knowing what poems meant and feeling stupid from school days. One friend enjoys repeating stanzas of poems including lyrics from hymns to herself while she goes about her daily chores. It's a good idea to have a poetry month to try and rekindle that childhood enjoyment of poems.

April 4: Important Peoples' Birthdays

Since I'm celebrating a birthday this month, I seem to notice others who were born in April. Today both Martin Luther King Jr. and Maya Angelou (two of my heroes) have birthdays. Their nonviolent work for social change inspires me. Every time I hear King's "I Have a Dream Speech" I tear up.

Some quotes from www.brainyquotes.com by Maya Angelou follow:
"I love to see a young girl go out and grab the world by the lapels. Life's a bitch and you have to go out and kick ass."
"I've learned that people will forget what you said, forget what you did, but people will never forget how you made them feel."

"I've learned you shouldn't go through life with a catcher's mitt on both hands. You need to be able to throw something back."

"Nothing will work unless you do."

"We may encounter many defeats, but we must not be defeated."

"I have found that among its other benefits, giving liberates the soul of the giver."

April 5: Many Birthday celebrations

I'm having a wonderful birthday month. The ingredients of a perfect birthday are lining up very well this year:
I've shared plenty of meals with friends, e-mails and phone calls from those I can't gather with, good weather for strolling and listening

to the chorus of spring birdsongs, and a homemade present here and there, including a hand-strung necklace, a jar of homemade salsa and dried banana and apple chips. Some spring sweaters to round out my wardrobe have me spruced up and ready for the Easter parade. A clean bill of health from the doctor, along with a tetanus shot should make me good for many years. I hope. I love having the time to savor gatherings and conversations with friends and look forward to the next one.

Maybe because I was a preemie and grew up knowing I was lucky to be alive, I have counted each year with joy—no being shy about my age for me. As Alexander Pope said:

"Pleas'd look forward, pleas'd to look behind, and count each birthday with a grateful mind." This year I'm particularly grateful for enough in so many areas of my life, wealth, health, friends, work, pleasure, and creature comforts. For next year I'd ask for more patience and more time!

April 6: Holidays and traditions

This weekend holds both the beginning of Passover and Easter. According to a recent survey over seventy percent of Americans celebrate a religious holiday this weekend and the other thirty percent probably can't avoid the marshmallow bunnies even if they try. I love the religious traditions of over two thousand years, but also enjoy the everyday parts like the lilies, and the Easter music. It's also fun to try the various food delicacies whether it's the lambs made out of butter, or someone's grandma's recipe for haroset. Since I didn't have any kids to dye eggs with this Easter, I guess I'll save them for deviling later.
Here are some cinquains I wrote for celebrating Passover, religious Easter and spring/Easter.

Pesach
God brings us through
The hard times and carries
Us forward to find new vistas.
Rejoice!

Easter!
God is with us.
Not in the tomb, away.

From our loss, our pain and joy..
Here now!

Easter
New beginnings
The new growth inside each
Person just like seeds in the ground
New hope.

April 7: Service

Helping fixing and serving represent three different ways of looking at life according to Rachel Naomi Remen, a wise physician who has written several wonderful books. When you help, you see life as weak. When you fix, you see life as broken. When you serve, you see life as whole.

Today I got to take pet food and supplies around to my twenty customers. We discussed spring weather, Easter plans, their animal's antics, and Fran's attempts to spot and threaten to chase cats. She doesn't even try very hard, knowing it is wrong. Just enough to say "I could but I won't." The volunteer I go with is a delight to serve with because she banters and chats, enjoys the animals, and lugs boxes of kitty litter without complaint. People are grateful, but we've been doing it long enough that it's the gratitude one has with a friend not the one down gratitude that one has with a charity.

April 8: Easter traditions

Some of my favorite parts of Easter have interesting origins. Take these for example:

Easter: the word comes from goddess of springtime in Anglo-Saxon mythology

Easter bunny: the goddess Eostre saved a bird whose wings had frozen by turning it into a rabbit.

Eggs: This bird/rabbit laid Easter eggs. Eggs were rare in winter but more plentiful in spring and a sign of fertility; hence a fine gift for this time of year. The first chocolate eggs were made in Europe about a hundred years ago.

Lamb: Eating lamb dates back to Passover celebration of angel of death passing by houses of Jewish people marked with blood of the lamb which the inhabitants had roasted and eaten. Christians called Jesus the Lamb of God; hence Jesus' sacrificial death is commemorated by eating lamb.

Hot cross buns: possibly started with wheat cakes eaten to celebrate goddess of spring; crosses added later by Christians

Lilies: symbols of resurrection; bulb symbolizes the tomb

April 9: National Library Week

I'm celebrating National Library Week by congratulating librarians on jobs well done, attending a poetry reading, and of course checking out plenty of books.

Because I'm blind and because when I was growing up so little was available in Braille or recorded, information access is extremely important to me. When I compliment librarians on jobs well done that means school librarians, public librarians, library for the blind staff, and Bookshare staff. Finding a book I want may mean checking several places to find it in accessible format.

Attending "Poets on Poetry" at my public library highlights another wonderful thing about libraries to me, they open doors free to worlds of ideas. There were poems about war, love, and topics in between. Some poems played with language in wonderful ways and comparisons were made by metaphors that made me think in new ways. These working poets were local people who donated their time. Many of them knew each other, so it was a community of poets sharing with the wider community.

As to checking out books, by Monday of National Library week, I'd read a book on Buddhism and was in the middle of a spy story from the public library and had downloaded five books on Easter traditions from Bookshare. No telling what horizons I'll explore by the end of National Library Week by borrowing from a library.

April 10: Why Apocalypse Now?

Having read one post-apocalyptic novel for a book club and another one to see if I could figure out why people like them, I'm getting curiouser and curiouser. The *Hunger Games* movie is taking the country by storm, and the books are on the best seller lists again. Is it just entertainment, and whatever sells that we see more of likes of the *Harry Potter* phenomena? Can we blame the media who need something to get our attention 24/7? Or, are our legitimate concerns about energy, the economy, and climate change leading to apocalyptic thinking of "Things can't keep getting worse, they'll have to end?"

All the way back to Old Testament times, the idea of the apocalypse has been around. The last big wave of apocalyptic thinking I remember was in the 1970's and was led by fundamental Protestants with books like *The Late Great Planet Earth* by Hal Lindsay. Nowadays we have another version where Mother Nature will rise up and set us straight.

But I wonder if we'll have a moment when everybody gets it (whatever the it is), or if we'll just keep muddling onward with trends toward higher gas prices, and bull markets followed by bear markets Maybe waiting for the apocalypse to set us straight is an escape, just like my beloved espionage thrillers. I hope people put limits on their consumption of apocalyptic lit, or nothing will get done to make the world better because, why bother if the end is near. I may need to add *The Last Myth* to my ever-growing list of must reads to understand this phenomenon better, but then again maybe I won't have to, it'll all become clear in a blinding? Moment of insight. If the alternatives are partying, praying or preparing for the apocalypse, I guess I'll continue praying about what to do right now and let God take care of the rest.

April 11: Graham Crackers' History and Shopping with Foodies

Today I took a road trip to a Trader Joe's, about an hour and a half from home, with two friends. One is quite a foodie. She collects cookbooks and has been to many cooking classes. She's been to the store several times, so led the charge, pointing out interesting samples and delicacies that we knew we wanted, like the rosemary raisin crackers (not a boring saltine by any stretch of the imagination.) My dad indoctrinated me early into the art of snooping a grocery store for international and interesting ethnic foods. I pre-shopped online so knew a few things to look at. If my long-suffering friends had had to name every-thing in the store, we'd still be there!

I ended up with Irish dark beer, chocolate covered almonds (chocolate from either Africa or South America), sushi, Indian tuna curry, and a chili mango frozen sorbet for dessert. As we rode home we talked about the change in American grocery stores from what we remembered growing up, just the basics, to this kind of world cuisine availability. I love to sample things like Trader Joe's chickpea and pasta salad and then figure out how to make it.

We also talked about the uses of food beyond just nutrition like entertainment. I got to enlighten my friends about the origin of graham crackers, a nugget of food trivia laid on my plate just yester-day. Rev. Graham was a minister in the eighteen hundreds who thought lustful thoughts were caused by a rich diet including meat. He recommended a vegetarian whole grain diet to stamp out those lustful thoughts, plus exercise, fresh air, no alcohol, and no tobacco. Fifty years after his death Nabisco had found the graham crackers, he had originated, were tastier when made with honey and now they're made with white flour. Now you know the cause of the ruination of American morals.

It was a fine trip to shop and hang with good friends; very ful-filling in many ways.

April 12: Pros and Cons of Aging

A friend on our county commission on aging interviewed me with the following questions. They are food for thought whatever one's age.

1. What do you think some of the pros of getting older are?
   Being able to share wisdom with younger people and hav-ing more free time to pursue   volunteer and leisure pursuits.

2. How about some of the cons, or challenges of getting older?
   Having l less energy to fight access issues; friends dying

3. What are the things you value that you don't want to lose as you get older?
   The ability to choose how I meet my needs and wants. Some people call this independence, but to me it's

interdependence with the choice about who, when, and why I depend on people.

4. What do you value that you expect to do more of as you get older? I don't expect to do more of anything than I am doing now; I've got a fine balance of work and play.

5. What do you see as an unmet need of for older people in Eau Claire County?

    Pet supplies for the "homebound" now met by small ECCHA program, but should be part of Meals on Wheels deliveries. Home teaching services for   newly blind and that possibly have other disabilities so they can stay in their homes. The State Office for the Blind is stretched too thin to do this meaningfully. Finally having reliable emergency transportation during the night (not ambulance. service)

April 13: Grateful? Lucky?

It's Friday the thirteenth and I'm concerned about a health issue for my guide dog. I'm not superstitious, but when someone I love is having problems, my mood declines quickly.

My first attempt to distract myself consisted of researching Friday the 13th and discovering that besides the movie, there was also a horror television series by that name. Upon further research, the idea that thirteen was bad luck seems to have become pervasive in the Middle Ages, when it was pointed out that Judas made thirteen at the Last Supper. Pagans sometimes have associated the number with the feminine as in thirteen moons in a year. Not that the patriarchy was always out to take shots at the feminine, but maybe this was part of the bad rap for thirteen. Of course it's a prime number and one more than twelve which is often regarded as a perfect number. Explaining life events by something we have no control over like an unlucky day, or bad omens dates back to ancient times. It's probably as good an answer to why bad things happen to good people as any, although I like the "If it doesn't kill you it makes you stronger" approach better.

I turned my mind to gratitude. Even if I don't feel it, maybe practicing it will help. Most basically, I have it all: food, shelter, safety, reasonable health, friends, interesting work, and time to spend on hobbies, and a relationship with a loving God.

Today I also checked in with a friend who has taken leave from work to be with a dying parent. She's savoring the momentary delights like birds at the feeder. Then, I checked my e-mail and found that something I introduced on a county committee is now done county-wide.

Finally, I immerse myself in Jeanette Winterson's memoir *Why Be Happy When You Can be Normal?* Like me, she grew up with family issues, has a longing to belong, and finds beacons of sanity in books.

When it all boils down, the old twelve-step slogan —one day at a time helps me fall asleep.

April 14: Was Jesus Happy?

Judging by bestselling books, Americans have a thing about happiness. Titles range from *Engineering Happiness* to *Choosing Happiness* to *Teach Yourself Happiness.*"

When the young person I'm sponsoring for confirmation sent me an article from Discovery about a cross-cultural study asking people whether they thought Jesus was happy, I was intrigued. I'd never even asked myself the question. My initial answer was "probably occasionally." My guesses as to the sources of his good feelings would be friendships and accomplishments when people occasionally "got" his message.

April 15: Spiritual Reading

As Henri Nouwen pointed out in *Bread for the Journey,* spiritual reading is different than reading for knowledge. It is "letting ourselves be mastered by the words" and opening ourselves to hearing the voice of God.

Sitting with a sentence rather than winning a speed reading contest is hard for me. When I'm doing spiritual reading or when my reading becomes spiritual, it brings me closer to a mystical union with God and others, not just knowing more about a subject. Missy Buchanan's thoughtful book on aging spiritually is a winner. Each year some of the essays in *Best American Spiritual Writing* do this for me, like the 2001 edition that I'm reading at the moment. Well written novels like *Cutting for Stone* by Abraham Vergheese or books by Lisa See, Barbara Kingsolver, Amy Tan, or Maeve Binchy take me to the hearts of characters and to the heart of a loving God.

April 16: Losing Mentors

Twice in the last month I learned of the death of dear friends who mentored me on my journey thirty years ago. Both were in their eighties and had lived long, full lives. I know they are at peace, with loved ones, and in no pain, but Lord I miss them. As I reach out to their friends and families, I'm aware of trying to say what they would have said or something in that spirit.

I haven't bookmarked the obituary page of the local paper on the Internet yet, but it might be about time. For a long time, the little kids I've talked to have considered me older than dirt, but I'm becoming an elder to their parents too. I don't have enough wisdom, enough compassion yet! There are so many questions I want to ask those older and wiser than me like how to gracefully make someone with cognitive decline feel valued in a conversation when they can't stay on topic anymore, or how to teach leaders to spend their last few years in the organization mentoring new leaders.

April 17: No Legacy; What Didn't I Do?

I had a unique experience at the Friends of the Library annual meeting tonight. Long ago, I was president of this group and was on the board or was the liaison with the board for at least six years. I'd asked if I could have the electronic handouts (reports from committees, biographies of people nominated for offices, etc.) ahead of time electronically but that didn't happen. Then the speaker for the meeting showed slides (or whatever they're called nowadays) of his trip for twenty five minutes with no commentary. I was out of luck for the whole meeting. A friend sat next to me and said "beautiful temples" descriptions occasionally. Afterwards the library director said something like "that wasn't very good for you was it?" I said I wonder if it should be announced on the program description that a program was to be silent and he said he didn't know. Talk about not getting it!

When I sent out a description of the situation to a blindness LISTSERV, I got lots of responses that many people have had similar situations again and again even with people and organizations they've educated before. Sometimes if they do something radical like handing out handouts only in Braille at a meeting, people get it for a while but then that awareness fades. Some suggest getting it as a requirement in the bylaws; some suggest screaming to the newspaper. Most seem to feel you keep educating again and again until the day you die or you give up and just don't go.

Nobody had much to say about slides with no description. The library director does want to put asking presenters about possible access issues on a checklist. I've offered to do a one-hour workshop for a few staff about how to narrate a program on the fly. We'll sit down with a very visual DVD with one staffer as narrator and the rest of us blindfolded for five minutes and then switch narrators. They won't be professionals when they are done, but they'll have an idea of how to do it. I've recruited a friend who is really a good describer to go along and model. Maybe she's good because she was a scientist in her career and used to noticing details.

April 18: Last Confirmation Class

Tonight I had the last confirmation class with my student. She'll be confirmed next month. I've learned so much each class; in some ways I'll miss the classes.

Tonight's was on prayer, so we discussed and demonstrated different ways of talking to and listening to God. In a guided meditation we were to imagine having dinner with Jesus, asking him a question and him giving us a gift.

All the students were given rosaries. I asked how you could say the Hail Mary's and at the same time think about the particular mystery you were supposed to be contemplating. The guy who answered said he got a picture in his mind's eye of the mystery and said the words "sort of a video channel and an audio."

My student told me the saint's name she has chosen for her confirmation name Katherine Drexel. She picked her because she had the same first name as me, and was into social action. My response to her was—"Good choice for your saint!"

Four things I like about Katherine Drexel (in addition to her first name):

She considered money she had as on loan to her and spent it on others;

She worked for education for minorities long before it was a popular cause;

She confronted discrimination;

She lived a long life (died at age 97).

I'll bet my student will enjoy having her covering her back.

April 19: Sociability

Today was a highly social day: lunch with friends followed by Scrabble Bee fundraiser for a local literacy organization. The friends were a gal my age and a gal in her eighties using a walker who also has several other medical issues. We slowly entered a restaurant with people holding doors and either waiting patiently or ducking around the procession with apologies. The walker user has such a pleasant aura surrounding her that everyone acted like it was their pleasure to wait. The other gal had a new car to show off with blue tooth which can make phone calls and change radio channels by talking to it. All of us were entranced. Fran enjoyed the conviviality and the car rides on a cool rainy day.

The event was for Literacy Volunteers of the Chippewa Valley, an organization that has helped 550 students this year. This is their main fundraiser. . There were table sponsors, twenty glorious baskets to bid on, and lots of friendly competition. Fran's Friends was again the only team in the Tortoise Division, playing regular Scrabble at our own speed, but we welcome competition next year. Fran's Friends raised the most money of any team, over $1830. Many people are fascinated each year with Scrabble in both print and Braille. Literacy for all! It was a nice event to end volunteer week with. Each person on the team volunteers in several places.

April 20: Garbage

I read the statistic that each American produces seven pounds of garbage per day. Yikes! In 2008 according to the Clean Air Council, the average amount of waste generated by each person in America per day was four and a half pounds. A little over one pound of that was recycled, and .4 pounds, including yard waste, was sent to composting. I don't know if it's gotten that much worse in five years, but in any case that's a lot. Plus we each use the equivalent of a hundred-foot-tall Douglas fir tree per year in wood and paper products according to the Clean Air Council. I think I'm worse than average on that one because of the Braille magazines I read and then put out for recycling. I was also shocked to learn half our food ends up as garbage. When I clean my fridge and throw out the green furry stuff I do feel guilty, but it happens every time. Then there are the plastic bags I use for picking up poop. The good news is that this is the second use of the bag, but they are still bad bags. What is a dog owner to do? I guess I'll just keep feeling mildly guilty until I find a better solution.

April 21: Being the Oldsters

One of the things I don't like about getting older is becoming part of the oldest generation. Within the last month, two dear friends and mentors in their eighties died. Both were "ready" so my sorrow is not for them but for me and other friends and family they left behind. I don't feel adequate to know the consoling things to say to their kids and grandkids. I listen and share a memory.

Today I learned a young adult family member has developed a potentially serious medical situation. How can I offer support and advice, but with a light touch? I'm not the parent but I am a senior family member.

Each of our relationships has a trajectory that death doesn't destroy. We see its arc in the inner changes we undergo when we remember deceased loved ones and even in outward changes as we continue to mold our lives in response to theirs.   -Patricia Campbell Carlson

April 22: Earth Day

"I love to think of nature as an unlimited broadcasting station through which God speaks to us every hour, if we will only tune in."
-George Washington Carver

"For the beauty of the earth;
For the glory of the skies
For the love which from our birth
Over and around us lies.
Lord of all to thee we raise
This our hymn of grateful praise."
-From a hymn by F. Pierpoint

April 23: Today's Project-A Letter about Accessible Prescription Drug Labeling

The Honorable Thomas Harkin
Chairman, Senate Committee on Health, Education, Labor and Pensions

The Honorable Michael B. Enzi
Ranking Minority Member

Dear Chairman Harkin and Ranking Member Enzi:

As one of the more than 21.5 million Americans living with significant vision loss, I am writing to congratulate you for reaching bipartisan agreement on the Food and Drug Administration Safety and Innovation Act. I am especially grateful that you have included language in the Manager's Amendment being considered this week which, once enacted, will lead to safer and more effective use of prescription medication by people who are blind or visually impaired.

As you know, people living with vision loss have consistently reported significant problems in the management of their prescription medications because drug container labeling is not accessible to them. In a survey conducted by the American Foundation for the Blind (www.afb.org/labels), people with vision loss indicate that retail pharmacies often refuse to offer container labeling that is independently readable by people who are blind or visually impaired; pharmacies are frequently simply unaware of the array of affordable low tech and high tech solutions available today to make container labeling more accessible. The legislation you are advancing would address this public health challenge through the development of national best practices in the delivery of accessible drug container labeling and evaluate use of such practices by retail and other pharmacies across the country through a Government Accountability Office report. We believe that, in addition to existing remedies available under the Americans with Disabilities Act and other federal and state law protecting the rights of people with disabilities, your legislation will go far toward helping pharmacies understand how they can best meet these existing obligations by implementing the most effective solutions.

I am hopeful that I and people like me won't have to continue distinguishing bottles by putting rubber bands on them (as in two equals take it twice a day). In 2012 we can do better! Again, thank you for your advocacy on behalf of people who are blind or visually impaired, I stand ready to assist you in moving this groundbreaking legislation through to the President's desk for signature.

Sincerely,
Katherine Schneider
Retired clinical psychologist
Eau Claire, WI

April 24: Sick at Heart

Ralph Waldo Emerson said "When it is dark enough, you can see the stars." Even metaphorically, this isn't working for me today.

Fran and I walked to the bank and she really had problems working when I was closer to the busy street than she was but did okay when she was between me and the cars. I can only think it's a vision thing. Seeing Eye hasn't told me when they'll send an instructor out to consult, although I requested it about ten days ago. Immediately would be perfect for me, but an organization with several thousand active graduates doesn't work that way, which I understand. I'm heartsick, off my feed, crying, and generally miserable. I fear Fran's retirement is coming soon. She'll make a wonderful pet. She's good with kids and seniors. I'd love to keep her but don't think I'd have the energy to keep her amused as well as work with the new dog. I also don't know what she'd think of sharing me. I've only had her three and a half years. It's so unfair. If there are any stars, they are a couple of friends who listen, care, and love both of us.

April 25: Memes and Other New Techie Words

The new meaning of the word "meme" - an electronic image passed around the Internet by sites like Facebook, makes me think sometimes I'm not missing much by not being able to see. Of course memes are not typically provided with an alt text tag describing them, so I miss out. And then there are emoticons which make no sense to me or my screen reader. Slightly more sensible are texting codes, for which there are online dictionaries like ChatSlang. Some of them are even funny like "tmi," and "tlidr." What did we ever do when we had to say "It was too long and I didn't read it" Or a better question, what are we doing with the time we gain by texting "tlidr?" Probably some are Facebooking the newest meme.

April 26: Never Happened and Never Should Have Happened

Sometimes I have a rush of envy for something I wish I'd said or written half as well as someone else did. Today it was title envy for Lawson's "mostly true" memoir *Let's Pretend This Never Happened*. Lawson's memoir of her bizarre upbringing in rural Texas, her devastatingly awkward high-school years, and her relationship with her long-suffering husband is her story, not mine. Oh I could have written some stories that would fit that title. Little funny ones, like saying "excuse me" to a post I accidentally bumped at the corner or going into the men's room instead of the women's right next to it On a much more serious note, I read today about the picture of a girl with Down syndrome that was turned into a meme called "I can count to potato" and splashed all over the Internet. Parents and other caring folk are trying to get this taken off Facebook. The damage is done and the young woman is mortified. She may be able to rise above it and make a funny story out of it someday, but it really never should have happened.

April 27: Arbor Day

Arbor Day was started in 1872 in Nebraska City, Nebraska and is now celebrated worldwide. I'm not planting any trees today, but I will be sure to stop and thank a couple of my favorite trees in the neighborhood, a couple pine trees with lovely soft needles.

Bill McKibben's over thirty years of environmental writing is inspiring to me. With his ideas of enoughness, and hundred dollar Christmas celebrations, he makes it seem possible to do something for this Earth we live on and enjoy. As he says "Now is the boomers' chance to reclaim their better, bolder natures and to end their run as it began." He thinks we should be leading the environmental movement, but that just isn't on my top five list currently. I'll reread a few of my favorites of his pieces and start *The Comforting Whirlwind* about the Bible and environmentalism.

April 28: Shock of Gray:

In *Shock of Gray,* Fishman discusses the implications of the fact that by the year 2030, one-billion people will be sixty-five or older. As the ratio of the old to the young grows ever larger, global aging has gone critical. For the first time in history, the number of people over age fifty will be greater than those under age seventeen. Are we seen as vulnerable, cherished, frail, kind, bothersome, sweet, expensive, wise, lonely, and irrelevant? Probably all of the above at various times, but a backlash against elders seems possible. In *Spiritual Teachings of the Avatar,* Armstrong points out that marginalizing the aging could be a societal response to this. Are the elders the new pariahs? What if technological medicine is able to push average longevity to one hundred years, while the world sees us as obsolete after sixty, or even fifty? Expectations swing between stay working as long as possible so we're not a drain on resources, but on the other hand we may need to get out of the way and let younger people have the jobs. We need to stay connected to the young, spending money and time on them so they'll like us. As a lobbyist friend of mine says: "If you're not at the table, you're on the menu."

April 29: Lots of Candles Plenty of Cake

As I read *Lots of Candles, Plenty of Cake* by Anna Quindlen, I loved many of her observations-like the necessity of girlfriends for the good life and the realization that the reason we forget things as we get older is that we have so many memories in our brains some just fall out. She says that "Along with the downsides of age, can come wisdom, a perspective on life that makes it satisfying and even joyful." A birthday party with a couple friends, one of whom always brings presents, complete with clues is a good example of this joyful attitude. We even danced to *klezmer* music with Fran. Quindlen quotes a birthday card that points out after the Middle Ages comes the Renaissance! Her last chapter is entitled "to be continued", and that's just how I feel about occupying my aging. I think we're soul mates.

April 30: Bucket List

George Elliot once said "It's never too late to be what you might have been."

With *Imagine* and *Wishes Fulfilled* on the best seller list and a book, television show, and website devoted to *What Do You Want to do Before You Die?* I've started working on my bucket list. So far my list includes: play audible darts, go to an audio described play, get into the fifty-year club at Seeing Eye, and give out the first disability journalism awards.

☽

May 1: Consequences of Making a Mistake on a Book Discussion List

Today, without giving a "spoiler alert" in the subject line, I revealed a plot element on a book discussion list. I was disemboweled and, it continued even after a contrite apology. Finally the list moderator weighed in as follows:

> I'm seeing unsubscriptions because some of us have blown out of proportion the fact that a reviewer accidentally mentioned the suicide of a character in a part of a book reviewed here. Unconscionable acts? Really list? Murder is an unconscionable act. Luring your unsuspecting guide dog into an industrial-strength blender is an unconscionable act. Inadvertently mentioning something about a character of a book is an accident, a tiny mistake that is neither unconscionable nor even particularly horrific when put in perspective.
>
> This list once prided itself on civility. We will get back to that if it requires every bit of energy I have to help make that happen.
>
> My co-moderator on this list has often accused me of revealing too much about a book's plot when I do reviews. Although he doubtless struggles with my reviews for that reason, I suspect my exuberance in talking about the plot has rarely left him dealing with sleeplessness or even outrage over an unconscionable act.

Now let's get it in perspective, shall we? The woman offed herself in that book. I've a hunch that's a fact anyone on this list could have stumbled onto. It was a tiny, tiny mistake on the part of the reviewer to mention that briefly without giving you warning—a warning that you might have inadvertently passed over despite the reviewer's best intentions! It was nothing more than that! This kind of yammering only serves to force people who might otherwise contribute reviews to have second thoughts or even to not do so at all. This thread is ended. We all get it—even clueless people like me who all too often reveals too much. I absolutely do not want to see any messages in which someone is taken to task with such vehemence over a tiny word or two in a review.

-Moderator

I think I learned not to do that again and I learned how seriously some people take what happens on a LISTSERV. I read them (or don't) but clearly take them with a bigger grain of salt than some do.

May 2: Clients of Nonprofits as Spokespeople vs. "Trained Monkeys"
"We've forgotten that a rich life consists fundamentally of serving others, trying to leave the world a little better than you found it. We need the courage to question the powers that be, the courage to be impatient with evil and patient with people, the courage to fight for social justice. In many instances we will be stepping out on nothing, and just hoping to land on something. But that's the struggle. To live is to wrestle with despair, yet never allow despair to have the last word."
-Cornel West, from The Impossible Will Take a Little While

I was a guest at a women's giving circle meeting where three nonprofits reported on what they'd done with the money they'd been given by the women's giving circle. Each of them had a client/customer to tell how much the service meant to them. The audience's heartstrings were suitably tugged and they said, "oh how wonderful" and clapped loudly. I was extremely uncomfortable and commented to a fourth nonprofit director who had not brought an appreciative client with her how much I appreciated her not doing that. She was torn because she's concerned that pulling heartstrings probably gets more money.

I'd like to do it better; pull heartstrings without exploiting recipients. I have been asked and have given those testimonials, but there has to be a better way. Ideas I solicited from a LISTSERV of people with disabilities I surveyed included videos with confidentiality protected and having volunteers talk. One person wrote:

> Are the nonprofits run and staffed by people from the same disability communities they serve? If not, the populations are being exploited/patronized twice over. To reverse this, people from these populations should run those nonprofits. In administrative positions, they get to decide how exactly to present themselves and their fellows who are their clients. Also, clients should be paid for their time when they present testimonials. If their presence and stories translate in more money, it's only fair that they do it professionally. That is, they know exactly what it's all about, have no illusions, and they know that they're performing. While pulling heartstrings, there will be many opportunities for them to subtly shift the rhetoric, make it hybrid, and discover ways to be effective wallet-openers and still honor their communities. Making clients partners can also lead to unique fundraising opportunities and get the nonprofit new networks of donors who are more enlightened. Just some thoughts!
> -John

May 3: Tough Day
Today, I sent the following e-mail to friends:

> The consultant from Seeing Eye left today. He recommended I retire Fran because her vision issue is affecting her work. I will do this, and at the moment, plan to keep her as a pet. I've never had a pet dog, so in retirement I feel this is a great time to give it a try. I've filed a replacement application with Seeing Eye but have no idea when I will be able to receive a new dog. A friend is taking us for an ophthalmology consult in Minneapolis on May 14. Of course if they came up with something a fixable

solution that would be an unexpected happy ending to this story, but at least I should get a prognosis. At this point Fran and I will work around the neighborhood as she and I feel it is safe. Thank you for caring.
-Kathie and Fran

I got back lovely, caring e-mails, a long phone call full of concern for both of us, an invite out for dinner, and a ride through the drive-through at the bank so Fran and I didn't have to walk there, which is no longer safe. By the end of the day I was beginning to think about where she could stay while I'm gone to training as well as other concrete next steps toward her retirement.

May 4: Moving Forward; Audio Describing
"Hope, O my soul, hope. You know neither the day nor the hour. Watch carefully, for everything passes quickly, even though your impatience turns a very short time into a long one."
-St. Teresa of Avila *The Way of Perfection*

Today I worked through some details of getting a new dog, like getting a physical arranged, and figuring out how to get it covered by insurance. Then I picked up supplies to deliver monthly pet food and boxes of kitty litter, and got advice on a good kennel for Fran to stay in while I'm gone for three weeks of training, whenever that is. People are being kind and helpful which is great since I feel my brain is only about half here.

I did get back to work on audio-describer training and came up with the following description and commandments for being an audio describer:

Seeing Out Loud: an Introduction to Audio Describing
Help the more than twenty-five million Americans who experience significant vision loss enjoy cultural opportunities more fully by becoming an audio describer! This one hour workshop will give you guidelines and practice opportunities in seeing out loud. Please bring sunglasses and a picture, object or DVD to share.

Nine Commandments of Audio Description
By Katherine Schneider, Ph.D.; schneiks@uwec.edu

1.   Something is better than nothing.
2.   Offer audio description; don't wait to be asked. "May I describe this for you?" is a good first line.
3.   Top priority goes to describing elements like plot details and to reading subtitles.
4.   Use vivid, descriptive words that are nonjudgmental. "Dirty" rather than "ugly." "Five story pagoda" rather than "pretty temple."
5.   Try not to talk when the speaker is talking, or when characters on screen are talking, but if it happens, just keep going.
6.   Don't waste words with "I'm seeing…" or personal comments like "I've never done this" or "I hate opera."
7.   Be careful about pronouns. "He got shot." Which "he"?
8.   If it's one to one description, try to check early on how this is for your listener.
9.   Your efforts are appreciated and you will get better the more you do. You may notice you "see more" even when not describing because of doing this work. That's your bonus!

May 5: Books I Wish Existed

The New York Times Book Review for April 15 started having a column called "By the Book," in which they'll ask famous people questions about their reading lives. In the first column, they asked author David Sedaris, what was the book he wished someone else would write. He replied he'd like to read a "non-hysterical biography of Michael Jackson."

A friend who has a deaf child suggested if she were still living, a memoir pointing out all the changes technology would have made in Helen Keller's life. Another friend suggested an updated *Walden*. Someone else voted for another Stieg Larsson mystery. I'd like a sequel to *The Shack*.

May 6: God's Heart Broke Too

It happened at church and luckily it was someone I love and I know loves me. His comment on Fran's retirement because of eye problems was: "You're sure hard on your dogs; they retire so quickly." When I told him my heart was breaking and his comment didn't help, he said, "just kidding." I told him I knew that, and I loved him anyway, but I had a favor to ask: if he heard anybody else say what he'd just said and he didn't think they loved me like he did, would he kick them in the nuts. He agreed he would.

I know as William Sloane Coffin said in a sermon about his son's death that God's heart "was the first of all our hearts to break" when tragedies happen. As he said God gives all of us "minimum protection—maximum support." I know this friend was trying to be supportive by teasing me. I hope this wasn't inoculation for somebody saying something worse.

May 7: Admiring Other Faiths

This is the week my confirmation student gets confirmed. Both she and I tend to admire other faiths instead of digging deep in our own.

To those who express an interest in living the simple life of the Amish, Saloma Furlong in her book *Why I Left the Amish* calls to mind something that has been quoted often in Amish literature, including in an issue of the *Small Farm Journal*: "If you admire our faith, strengthen yours. If you admire our sense of commitment, deepen yours. If you admire our community spirit, build your own. If you admire the simple life, cut back. If you admire deep character and enduring values, live them yourself."

May 8: Voting

Voting is a sacred privilege to me. Not until the Help America Vote Act of 2002, not fully realized until 2006, did I ever have a secret ballot. Before that I had to ask a friend to read me the choices and I told them which to mark, or I had to have a Republican poll official, and a Democrat poll official with me in a booth so one could mark my ballot and the other could watch them. I'm sure they were honest and kept my confidence, but it just didn't feel like a secret ballot. Now I use a set of headphones and a little thing like a television remote to mark my choices on the "handicapped" voting machine. The first time I voted by myself, I cried. Now I was a real American.

So every chance I get, I vote. Sometimes the "handicapped" machine doesn't work right and has to be fixed and sometimes I still have to go back to having a friend help if the machine is really surly, but I vote because I can.

Today the synthetic speech was done wrong so it announced the ballot as Republican gubernatorial primary when it was both Republican and Democrat. You could get to the Democratic candidates but it was done misleadingly. Now I have to figure out how to complain. I asked about it on some blindness LISTSERVs in the state and one person said they just gave up and didn't vote because it was done wrong. I will howl long and loud about this. I wasn't looking for another project, but I am morally bound to take this on. If we don't use our freedom and make sure it's there for others, we can't complain if it goes away.

May 9: Loch Ness Monster in Local River Story

A couple weeks ago some group of people made a sculpture of the Loch Ness monster and placed it in the Chippewa River. After a few days the Department of Natural Resources said it didn't meet rules and had to be removed. It was. Now the same anonymous group of people has put another Nessie there, bigger and better!

According to the Facebook page of our local alternative newspaper, *Volume One*:

> The saga continues! The artist(s) responsible for the Loch Ness Monster statue… created a brand new, better, faster, stronger Nessie and placed it in almost the same spot as the original one. We just noticed it back this morning. A quick e-mail to the anonymous Nessie-maker produced the following reply:

> There is a new Loch Ness Monster in the same spot now. We redesigned the new one to float like a raft – it is chained to the bottom and is setup to raise and lower up to 10 feet with the changing water levels. It has 9 small reflectors around the raft a red one for her eye. She is built to float sideways in low water and straight down river in high water. Due to high waters she's

not as far out as she was before, we will move her out further once the water goes down. We used the same mold pattern as the first Nessie. Not sure if it's still legal with the DNR. If it's not maybe we can change it to be legal. I'm sure they will let us know. We want to thank all of you for your great comments. The first Nessie is doing fine we are looking for a new place for her because she's afraid of that darn DNR.

The Phoenix

(The Phoenix is group of guys just having some fun with art)

Following our own Nessie is brightening my week and I think that of a lot of other people. A good use of artistic creativity!

May 10: Nessie Update and Enjoying a Quiet Day

According to this morning's newspaper, the Department of Natural Resources says the new Nessie isn't legal either. The crafters of Nessie, the owner and workers at a local cement plant have come forward. The saga continues.

After yesterday's nine hours of meetings and talking with at least thirty-five people, it was a relief today to only have an hour and a half of meetings and talk to twenty people or less. I worked on the voting problem and got as far as I could—a call from the Disability Rights Wisconsin's lawyer's secretary to do an intake taking my complaint and saying they'll call me Monday. Eau Claire Democrats haven't called back yet. I want them to care but they may not.

May 11: Confirmation: "We are a Pilgrim People"

After a dinner with my confirmation student's family, we went to a local church and had a two-hour confirmation service. The bishop's homily was thirty-five minutes long. A summary could be: Jesus is alive. Call on the Holy Spirit to give you courage to be Christian in the world. He asked confirmands questions in such a way they were really not sure if it was an easy question or a trick question. I was interested that he talked about their doing great things in education and being captains of industry, but mentioned vocations to religious life and parenthood as kind of afterthoughts.

I wish he'd shared some of his faith journey, quoted Richard Paul Evans' *Road to Grace*, or otherwise given us all something to remember other than we got through it.

And we didn't even sing John Henry Newman's, "Lead Kindly Light" although maybe they thought that was too gloomy.

Afterwards we went out for ice cream-my treat- and chatted. I'd given my student a statue of St. Francis and she gave me a necklace with my initial, hers, and Fran's in Braille with little stones on it. I wonder how we'll share the journey as the years go by.

May 12: Grace

Richard Paul Evans in the third part of his walk series, *The Road to Grace* talks about grace being all around us. Grace is one of those churchy words I never thought much about until I passed middle age. Somehow nowadays, favor, mercy and effortless ease (dictionary.com's meanings for the word) seem lovelier. Today I noticed unmerited kindnesses from friends, birds moving quickly and quietly from one place to another and the basic grace of having another day on this earth with enough food, enough work and enough rest. Even though the song "Amazing Grace" is not one of my favorites because of that line "was blind but now I see, "otherwise it would be a good one to hum as I walk through a grace filled day like today.

May 13: Mother's Day

"A mother is not a person to lean on, but a person to make leaning unnecessary."
-Dorothy Canfield Fisher

Richard Rohr in a talk on the maternal face of God, talks about the maternal parts of God being grounding, intimacy, trust, and safety. As I reflect back to the gifts my mother gave me, grounding is one of the biggest. Grounding is the realization that life is a struggle; you have to give 110 percent effort and that God gave you a brain—so use it! Mom also gave me a love of reading, especially international intrigue.

Tomorrow at Red Hats we'll show and tell something about our moms. I'll take a figurine of a camel and talk about mom's achieving something on her bucket list when she rode a camel in Egypt on a tour she took, by herself, through a local college when she was over fifty and figured my brother and I could survive without her for a few weeks. Go for it, moms of the world and thanks for the gifts you gave us, starting with life itself.

Another mom I admire immensely is Barbara Johnson. When I'm down I love to dip into one of her books like *Living Somewhere Between Estrogen and Death* or *Humor Me, I'm Over the Hill* She manages to make a funny story out of life events but still care and be Christian. Reeve Lindberg and her mom, Anne Lindberg, make a fun combination to read on Mother's Day.

May 14: Fifty Shades of Gray

I read *Fifty Shades of Gray* for three reasons: prurient curiosity, intellectual freedom, and to be "in."

It has no literary merit, little plot, many descriptions of sex practices, and if I hadn't skipped and skimmed, I'd really think I wasted my time. It reminds me of the inane television they have on in some airports, but with sex descriptions added. You don't mind at all if your plane gets called and you have to leave in mid story. I read all three books in the series, not believing the second and third could be as bad as the first. They were! The only good news is I got them from a library, so I didn't spend money, just time. But I'm having fun regaling friends who won't read them with how bad they are. Prurient pleasure of the second order I guess.

May 15: Getting to Second Base Sometimes

Today I did the audio describer training for ten people: librarians and a couple gals from local museums. They seemed to have fun, get something out of it and leave feeling they could do it or at least try. One gal had to tell me how she always reads *Seven Blind Men who Went to See the Elephant*. I shared with her that it evoked painful memories for me of when that was taught when I was growing up and kids later calling me stupid because I didn't know what an elephant looked like. All she heard was I knew the book, which confirmed to her that she was doing a great thing. No home run with her, but others got something.

The Women's Giving Circle leadership has met and will restructure so that grateful recipients won't be paraded quite so obviously. This news came to me with a nudge to join committees to help make it better. I probably will, with a sigh in my heart. If you want change, I know you have to be the change, but I'm feeling weary.

There's still no action on the audible ballot, so tomorrow I'll have to push that project.

May 16: It's So Daily!

I finally talked to the lawyer about the accessible voting problem and gave her the names of three others who had the same problem in different towns. I got a decent ad written and sent to dog people about being willing to consider other retirement options for Fran. Then it was time to go to the ADRC board and then the church celebration of my student's confirmation. In both places I experienced some invisibility; e.g. people talking to the person next to me not me. When I returned home, I read an article in the May 9 *New York Times* about elder invisibility and I groaned. If I'm already invisible because I'm blind, older and blind should be a real trip. Is there more invisible? I guess I'll find out.

In one instance I managed to give the person some feedback because she was in a work role and I could do it as feedback about how to do her job "even better." She got it and at least said she appreciated it. In social situations all I usually do is answer the questions they put to my companion, and then ask them something back to try to get them to respond directly to me. I can get annoyed, or on better days play it like a tennis game: how many volleys does it take.

May 17: Graduation/Retirement Advice

In some ways graduating and retiring are similar: they're transitions that are both exciting and scary, and they call for celebrating and pontificating. Here's a description I wrote shortly after I retired of what it's like:

> Retirement seems to be a time for doing new things and enjoying picking up some old ones. In the former category, last week I blogged, picked blueberries, went to a political party and a mission dinner for an AIDS mission in Haiti. In the latter category, I'm enjoying cooking slow food, some from the local farmers' market, and reading novels. I finished *The Fountainhead* by Ayn Rand that my younger nephew had been after me forever to read and just started an English mystery, *Agatha Raisin and the Vicious Vet*. The vet gets bumped off early on but

I don't have a clue whodunit yet. This week I went up for an overnight on Madeline Island in Lake Superior with a friend at their summer home. My Seeing Eye dog wishes to report that the weeds at the blueberry patch were more interesting than the berries and that she's enjoying more walks and fewer meetings. She rated Lake Superior as "awesome."

The advice I'll give my friend who is retiring is to try lots of things, but don't commit to anything for about six months. If he's anything like me, he'll do the kid in the candy store thing and if he signs on to all the fun opportunities for education, service, socializing and relaxing, he'll be exhausted and have to retire from retirement. People always told me they were busier after they retired, than when they worked, and I didn't believe them. It is true, but the choice of doing it or not is the best part. There are plenty of books out there to help you deal with the finances, decisions about where to live, and even a few for couples on how to negotiate being together full time.

In three words, live it up!

May 18: Beau Geste Effect

Today I heard a program on wolves talking about the Beau Geste Effect. It means that a two wolf pack makes the same amount of howl as a bigger pack, fooling other packs into thinking it's a bigger pack. There's got to be a practical use of this bit of information other than if I'm alone in a forest not being unduly frightened by a big sounding pack, but I don't know what it is. It's just fun to learn something new for no good reason sometimes.

May 19: Third Act and Gardening

Today I listened to a TED talk by Jane Fonda about our third act, aging. She said to think of life as staircase, where our spirits keep ascending rather than an arch, where aging is declining into decrepitude. She said a third of how we age is determined by genetics and the rest is attitudes and actions. She recommends a life review and forgiving yourself and others. Then her point seemed to be, do what the spirit leads you to do.

Some friends of mine stopped by to help plant my garden, bringing radishes, sweet potatoes, tomatoes, a petunia, and some sunflower seeds. The man is a permanent wheelchair user and his wife is four days away from a knee replacement. I was the second of three stops on their planting tour. Makes you humble.

I turned on the news and heard of a seventy-three year-old woman climbing Mount Everest. I guess she'd buy into the staircase analogy!

May 20: Proverbs

The Beliefnet e-mail of the day was about proverbs and this got me thinking about favorite proverbs. A couple of mine are "waste not, want not" by Ben Franklin, and "something is better than nothing,"(author unknown).

Wiseoldsayings.com even has a list of wise new sayings like: "action is the antidote to despair," by Joan Baez. When I did an unscientific survey of friends and LISTSERVs, I got the following:

"The road to a friend's house is never long."
-Danish Proverb

"We have not inherited this land from our ancestors; rather we have borrowed
it from our children."
-African Proverb

"If you think you have someone eating out of your hands, it is a good idea to
count your fingers."
-Nigerian Proverb

"Don't worry about the world coming to an end today. It's already tomorrow in
Australia."
-Charles Schulz

"I think remorse ought to stop biting the consciences that feed it."
-Ogden Nash

"It ain't what they call you but what you answer to."
-W.C. Fields

"A house divided against itself cannot stand."

"A man wrapped up in himself makes a small package."

"A man's best friend is his dog."

"Patience is a virtue."

"To err is human, to forgive is divine."

May 21: The Sound of Music

I was reading *The World in Six Songs: How the Musical Brain Created Human Nature* by Daniel Leviton today. He posits that songs of friendship, joy, comfort, knowledge, religion and love helped us become as civilized as we are. Americans spend more money on music than on prescription drugs and we hear, on average, about five hours a day of music. It is the soundtrack of our lives. Just try to say the alphabet without humming the alphabet song. I can usually get through readings and sermons at funerals, but when the piano or organ starts up with a grand old hymn, I'd better have a handkerchief ready.

In the spring, especially, I'm reminded that we're not the only ones whose lives are structured by songs. The birds set territory, find mates, and communicate with their babies as well as call alarms by their songs. I'm convinced that even my beloved crows, although not considered song birds, do try to sing. Thank God for songs of the wild and human-made songs.

May 22: How to Decide

A friend was telling me about several friends who are going through crises trying to decide what to do in retirement. A young friend is trying to decide whether to stay at home and raise her child (who has disabilities) or get a low-paying job and use the money to pay for day-care while she works. I'm trying to decide on the best retirement scenario for my guide dog.

I'm used to the kind of decision-making where you list the pros and cons of each choice and the decision becomes obvious fairly quickly. I was reading *The Jesuit Guide to Almost Everything*. Now, I've added another piece: what harm can come of each choice?

May 23: Funerals, Memorial Services, and Celebrations of Life:

When one leaves for the stars, that person will be the one to blink at you in the night-sky and show you the way. While s/he will no longer be able to touch your hands s/he will forever be able to touch your heart.
-Karla A. Claeys, M.A

I went to a really well-done celebration of a friend's life. The minister's talk was down-to-earth and showed that he knew and liked the person. On his last visit, she'd been doing a jigsaw puzzle, and they talked about how she'd put the pieces of her life together. He talked using that analogy. The church was almost full with neighbors and some of the children's coworkers. Of course, the luncheon afterwards was complete with fond memories and homemade bars. Even though the body went to science, she was wise to give her mourners this gift of a place and time to publicly grieve.

May 24: Older People Are Happier

Another study just came out reporting that older people on average are happier than younger people. Some reasons they missed: senior discounts; reading the obits and realizing you're not there; no need to buy feminine products or birth control; you know you will live through heartbreak; there's a name for forgetting things, and "senior moments" sounds better than "space case."

May 25: Audism, *Curious Incident* and Blind Movie Reviewer

Three media pieces reminded me today that we each experience life from our own perspective, and aren't even aware of it until another viewpoint is raised. I read a post on a Disability Studies e-mail list complaining about American Heritage Dictionary's definition of audism. It means favoring the hearing perspective on things. I finished reading *Curious Incident of the Dog in the Night* about life from the viewpoint of a young man with Asperger's syndrome. *USA Today* had an article about a movie reviewer who was blind.

The reality of these different perspectives became clear to me when I heard people discussing an acquaintance, who it seemed, had bipolar disorder, and another who struggles with alcohol issues. The discussions ranged from laughing at how oddly they behaved, to being angry about their behaviors. It made me ache inside, thinking how lonely the people with the mental illnesses probably felt. In both conversations, when I threw in something about the person having a mental illness and how alienated they must feel, the topic switched. I don't know if future interactions will be any more productive, or if they just won't mock their acquaintances in front of me.
The conversation moved on to knocking someone who was having a lot of issues with memory loss. When I mentioned that most of us, including me, have some of those issues and laughed at one of my own, the subject was dropped. I'm okay with laughing with somebody *about* an issue we share but not laughing *at*. Honoring differences, empathizing, learning from, laughing with, and enjoying the differences all take more time and energy than just saying, "they're weird," I know, but the former sure feel better than the latter on the receiving end. Viva la difference!

May 26: Bombshell!

Suzanne Somers's latest book is on aging and is called *Bombshell.* It's all about how we can reverse aging now and in the future. Her suggestions range from exercising (yoga, strength, and cardio), taking a warm bath every night, and eating organic foods to taking supplements, using hormone creams, and using nanotechnology patches for pain. Mental parts of the regimen include imagining your goal for how you want to be as you age, researching and choosing the right doctor to work with you, and figuring out how to avoid toxins. Although studies and doctors are liberally quoted, her plan seems far-out to me. She's used to hearing this, though, and points out that it's important to figure out what you're comfortable doing or trying and then go for it. I think I should pull out that old yoga book I have and get busy with it, maybe in the fall.

May 27: Pentecost

Mass for Pentecost came complete with a rushing wind, storm sirens, and a downpour when it was time to leave church. I find myself wanting a rushing wind to blow me in the right direction from the Holy Spirit instead of the still, small voice that is much more common in my experience, anyway.

I'm asking myself if I'm moving out in faith or just standing still. This week, I'll try to get a story on local television to see if a better home than mine can be found for Fran. Am I focusing on hope beyond this dark time? Am I reaching out in love to those around me, or sulking that they don't love me right?

"Create in me a clean heart," as the psalm says.

May 28: Most Beautiful Words

The June 2012 *Reader's Digest* had quotations from a few notable people for finishing the sentence, "The most beautiful words in the English language are: …"

Dorthy Parker: "Check enclosed."

President George H. W. Bush: "Play ball!"

Gore Vidal: "I told you so."

My answers are: "I love you," "welcome home," and "thank you."
Friends who took it to mean beauty in the actual word suggested "melancholy" and "majestic."

May 29: Asperger's Syndrome Novels

I've read three of the dozens of novels out there now about people with Asperger's Syndrome, a high-functioning form of autism. *Unlocked: a Love Story* by Karen Kingsberry tells the story of how a teen with autism and his family are somewhat healed by music and God's love. *The Curious Incident of the Dog in the Night* describes the struggles of a teen to solve the mystery of the killing of a dog and move forward in his own life. *House Rules* by Jodi Picoult tells of a family's trauma when their autistic son is suspected of committing a murder. I just wonder how realistic they are from an Aspie's viewpoint.

May 30: Joan of Arc and Finding a Brailler for an Adult Student

Today, the feast of Joan of Arc was celebrated. She was a woman of conscience who tangled with authorities because she was on a mission. She's one of my heroes.

It seems appropriate that I'm working several angles to get an adult, newly-blind person a Braille writer. The price tag for this ten-pound piece of equipment (sort of like a typewriter, but with fewer keys) is $650 new. At any given time there are several on eBay, but sellers usually are not the blind person who used it but a relative who is clearing out grandma's house and has no idea if it works. If it were for a school-age child, the school would buy it. If the person was a veteran, the Veterans Administration would. If the person is likely to be employable, Vocational Rehabilitation might. Since the person I'm helping is none of the above, however lives on a very limited income, and just wants to learn how to read and write so that they can jot down phone numbers, no government programs apply. I was able to get the local literacy organization to agree to buy the braille writer if I get the money donated to them. That way, generous donors can report it as a charitable donation. It's only taken a couple of hours to get this all organized. Now I can fundraise.

May 31: *Wonderstruck*—not!

By a Herculean effort, the National Library Service for the Blind got *Wonderstruck*, a largely graphic novel that won the Schneider Family Book Award, audio-described and recorded within four months. The narrator did a good job of briefly describing the over four-hundred pages of pictures that told half the story. The novel involved two deaf children, fifty years apart, both touched by the Natural History Museum in New York.

With great effort, both storylines were made clear. Blind children (but not deaf blind children, because the book was recorded) can read it. To me, it's an okay story, but I'd be hard-pressed to know why it won any award. It's about as exciting as hearing that there's a red and pink sunset with a bank of gray clouds moving in. Sometimes a picture is worth a thousand words and that's just how it is. I'm sad at what I'm missing, not wonderstruck.

☽

June 1: The Wonders of Dogs

As I try to get the local media interested in doing a story on Fran's retirement, I think a lot about how special she is and how much love she has to give. A single mom with a two year-old has expressed interest, but she works all day and I don't think Fran would react well to being alone that much. I'm reading *Until Tuesday*. It's about an Iraq war veteran and his golden Retriever service dog. Could she move to that career where her vision would not be that important? Then, out of the blue, I start getting e-mails from a veteran with a service dog that is having many access fights. My heart goes out to him. He fought for this country and now faces discrimination instead of thanks. I'm trying to cheer him on by e-mail. That's all I can do. I occasionally have those fights, even though there have been guide dogs for over eighty years. Service dogs are a much newer phenomenon. Dogs give so much love. How can people not want them around!

June 2: Creating the Dance

"The Invitation," a prose poem by Oriah Mountain Dreamer, has always impressed me. In her book, *The Dance,* she talks about how to live in a way that is consistent with our longing to discover a gift that we can give ourselves again and again.

A woman who helps me deliver pet food is a modern dancer. We were talking about creating a dance and I asked her about what comes first. She said that for one of her teachers the costume comes first, then the theme, the dance, and the music last. For another teacher, music is first and costume last. My young friend had a piece of music in mind to dance, but she said the choreography was coming out too literally that way, not modern enough.

According to Thomas Merton, "It is true that we are called to create a better world, but we are, first of all, called to a more immediate and exalted task: that of creating our own lives."

I was never big on dancing having suffered through a few years of ballroom dance lessons as a child. We all create the dance of our lives; it is a beautiful dance because it is unique.

June 3: The Joy of Children's Books

I think I have a new favorite children's book to add to my short list: *Pete the Cat: I Love My White Shoes,* by Eric Litwin. Its message of "keep singing your song" is good for those of us occupying aging as well as for kids. My short list of favorites tends to run to animal books like *Winnie the Pooh, Aesop's Fables, Wind in the Willows,* and the *Velveteen Rabbit.* My first favorite book was *The Little Engine That Could.* Its motto of "I think I can, I think I can" has been the driving force in my life as I look back. Maybe that and "keep singing your song" will carry me through the rest of my life, or maybe a new favorite children's book is just around the corner.

June 4: Becoming a Centenarian

The number of American centenarians has roughly doubled in the
past twenty years to about 72,000. Today, I think I'd like to become one. Sooner than that, there's another club I'd like to join, Seeing Eye graduates who have worked with Seeing Eye dogs for fifty years. Right now, I've got thirty-nine years in, about two thirds of my life! Even with all the hard parts like retiring dogs, I still hope to do this. Probably the same activities will help me achieve both goals: exercise, eating well-balanced meals, keeping intellectually stimulated, and socially engaged. Many elders seem to have the positive attitude of making lemonade out of lemons down to a fine art. Nowadays, that's a stretch for me, but I'm stretching, and groaning and stretching.

June 5: Entertaining

Today, friends came by for coffee on the patio and my nephew and his family (complete with two-year-old and seven-year-old) came to visit for lunch and an afternoon at the Children's Museum. In my clean up, I found only a few things that they left behind. As soon as Fran ate and went out to potty, she went to bed. I don't know how grandparents raise grandkids. I'm ready for a rest after only half a day. Of course, they're priceless, and I love seeing them. I told each child that they could pick an animal out of a bag of Beanie Babies that I was holding. The two-year-old picked my dog as his animal. They are sweet, smart, wonderful kids, and well parented. The older one even said "thank you" once.

June 6: Assuming

Today, I started the day by getting a physical to complete the requirements for my Seeing Eye application. The sweet young nurse filled out lots of screens of information for their records and told me that she was marking that I needed assistance cooking, bathing, and dressing, right? I said, "No" and she exclaimed, "Don't you have a caregiver?" I told her, no, unless you counted Fran and we took care of each other. Amazing!

Later in the day, I got an e-mail from Seeing Eye about new regulations from the transportation and security administration (TSA) regarding assistance animals, including requiring that we hold on to the leash at all times (but not the harness) until the animal has been searched. Now they've added a requirement that we have our hands be wiped with a rag to check for explosive residue. This is in addition to the hand search, the wand search, and the enhanced (crotch and butt crack) search. I just hope I don't get confused and think they're going to wipe my butt for me with that rag. They even have a new "TSA Cares" line in case we need further explanations of their procedures. I do appreciate their care that no passenger blow up an airliner, but how many guide dog bombers have there been?

I've gone from someone assuming that I need my butt wiped, to TSA assuming that I'll blow up a plane today. It reminds me of that old saying, "to assume makes an ass out of you and me."

June 7: Live Life!

The morning newspaper had an article about a group of UW-Stout students authoring an anthology called *Live Life* to benefit the American Cancer Society. I'm reading Burroughs's anti-self-help book *This Is How*. In his humorous style, he talks about being yourself, warts and all, and living life, not psychoanalyzing it. It's good advice as I wait for responses to my posting of Fran's need of a home on one television station's website, and a story airing this evening on the other local station.

Fran and I practiced walking to the art class I'm starting next week, and she did fine. After we left the building, we walked out the door and almost into a truck parked by the door. Fran trotted right up to the workmen standing by the truck fully convinced that they were there to give us a ride home. After I told her, "No, we'll walk," we ambled home. She does look for the best solution to her problems!

A book arrived in the afternoon mail, *Power Thoughts* by Joyce Meyer. That kind of book is exactly what Burroughs is laughing at. I took a quick peek at the dozen power thoughts she recommends, and on good days, I can at least attempt most of them. "I am difficult to offend" gives me pause.

God gave me practice. The piece on Fran was not aired by the local television station today. The governor was in Chippewa Falls, and some tree leaves had holes in them, so she was aced out by those stories, I guess. Perhaps tomorrow, I hope.

June 8: Fran's Story Continues

Just to make sure I kept working on the not-easily-offended piece, I got the following e-mail response to the short article on WQOW's website:

"How dare you throw this animal away just because Fran develops a problem similar to yours? YOU should give Fran a wonderful retirement for all the time this devoted animal has given to you."

It felt like a hard kick in the gut. Ten out of ten friends I ran it by said, "Don't respond," or, "Go for the jugular," or "Let me!"

After a lot of thought and prayer, I decided to respond. I claim to be a Christian, and I represent guide dog users. Ideally, she will never do this to someone else with a service dog. I said:

You and I agree Fran deserves only the best because of all the hard work she has done. If nobody comes forward who will give her a better home than I can, I will gladly keep her. You misjudge the depth of love and care I have for her. Retiring a guide dog is the hardest thing I have ever done and

since they don't live as long as people do, I have done it several times.

In each case I have found a wonderful retirement home for the dog. I hope you take your deep caring about animals and use it to help at your local shelter or such.

And she responded:

> I work with therapy horses, special needs students, do research (FOIA, OPRA for a national animal protection organization), and rescued my cats from a parking lot. Bought my thorough-bred solely to save her from slaughter. I am very active in animal welfare. Banning horse slaughter is my mission. And, I am appalled at the sham journalism that passes for news. Working hard to be a voice for innocent animals. Vegetarian. Thank you for responding.

I wonder how my fellow vegetarian treats the people with disabilities with whom she does therapeutic riding classes. I'll let it rest.

June 9: Responses to Fran's Television Appearance

I got about twenty-five responses to Fran's bid for a new home. They ranged from rural to city people. Physicians volunteered, and so did people living on disability income. Offers came from people with four kids or five dogs and from people who have been without a dog for a few years and now are ready to have a new four-legged family member. Some dropped out when they found that they'd have to take her out every four hours, but some stayed in the running.

A man with a brain tumor and his wife came by for a nice long visit. They are really nice people and Fran warmed to them right away. We discussed my concerns and I answered their excellent questions. We took a walk, with the man walking Fran and me taking the wife's arm. She teaches second grade in Minnesota, so Fran and I autographed a copy of *Your Treasure Hunt* and they were both thrilled with it. They're going to talk and let me know if they're interested. If they are, they'll land near the top of my list.

Initially, I didn't even want to meet them, fearing Fran would be just an added burden. It was a good reminder to me to let the process work. It's exhausting work.

June 10: Pulling Out my Psychological First Aid Kit

Today, I needed some psychological first aid, so I mentally went through my kit: friends, books, nature, music, prayer, poetry, and chocolate sprung immediately to mind. I felt the need for some poetry. As Matthew Arnold says, poetry teaches us "how to live." *Ten Poems to Last a Lifetime,* by Roger Housden, and his whole series of *Ten Poems* books are great places to start. A little Ogden Nash to lighten things up always helps. By the end of the day, all items in the first aid kit had been used and the patient felt much better. There was still most of the package of M&Ms left for another day!

June 11: Retirement Goals

A friend who is just retiring sent out, along with the invitation to his retirement party, his list of retirement goals: some reading, learning new subjects, learning a language, getting back to playing the banjo, etc. Wow! He is a brainy person who clearly plans to keep the gray matter busy.

So many projects jump up and bite me that I have trouble making any progress on those few small goals that I set out on January 1st. It'll be fun to talk to him in a year and find out how much he's accomplished.

But first, the party!

June 12: Fran Again

Three days after the television story, Fran had e-mails from over twenty-five people. Over one-hundred people recommended the story on the television website and eleven people commented on the site. Some of the suggestions people made were; that I take her back to Seeing Eye, get her eye fixed, give her to someone as a therapy dog, and keep her myself. I thought about posting that I'd considered all of the above. Maybe Fran needs a blog.

Four hours after our second interview, I was able to write people:

Fran will be going to live with Rae, a gal about my age who lives on the north side of Eau Claire. She and Fran are already planning nice walks where Fran gets to sniff around and ice cubes as treats when they get home from the walks. Car rides, nursing home visits and time spent enjoying each other's company is also in the works. Rae understands that Fran won't move until I go to Seeing Eye and we don't know when that will be. Thanks for rooting for us through this process.

    Kathie and Fran

Friends e-mailed back asking if Fran got a signing bonus and saying they'd light a candle for us. Of the ten seriously interested to whom I sent the update, all but one wrote back gracious e-mails. Both television stations want to claim credit for having found her a home, so I needed to send diplomatic e-mails to them as well.

I end the day relieved that Fran has found a good home. I'm sad that it's become more real to me that she will go. I'm scared about whether I can do it again; especially forming the bond with Young and Foolish (what I call the new dog until I get it).

June 13: If I Texted

There are senior texting codes (which are tongue in cheek) like the following:

ATD = At the Doctors
BFF = Best Friend Fell
BTW = Bring the Wheelchair
BYOT = Bring Your Own Teeth
FWIW = Forgot Where I Was
GGPBL = Gotta Go, Pacemaker Battery Low
GHA = Got Heartburn Again
IMHO = Is My Hearing-Aid On?
LOL = Lots of Lipitor
OMMR = On My Massage Recliner
OMSG = Oh My! Sorry, Gas
ROFLACGU = Rolling on Floor Laughing and Can't Get Up
TTYL = Talk to You Louder

Reading these caused me to think of codes blind people might use. One that I've actually read is ABAPITA (Ain't Blindness a Pain in the Anatomy!) My list of blindness texting codes so far:

AFPA = Accessible Format Please, Again!
WTHIT = What the Heck is This? (Useful in refrigerator cleaning.)
WIT = Where is "There?"
WTHAI = Where the Heck Am I?
WWT = Who Was That?
WDYMOT = What Do You Mean, "Over there."

I'd bet every disability could use a few of these short-hand phrases.

June 14: To Quit Art Class or Not to Quit

I rarely dropped classes when I was a student. Now I'm strongly considering dropping Ceramics after about a third of the class. I'm slow to learn physical skills like dancing, swimming, or in this case, throwing on a pottery wheel. The only way I learn is to have someone guide my hands to where they need to be several times, and then verbally cue me through it repeatedly, and then back off.

In this class, there are eighteen students. The teacher tries to verbalize what she's doing in her demos, but tonight the "you take this" and "do that" became too much for me to even try new skills. I was playing on the wheel and turned one lump of clay out of seven into a pot. The teacher said it took her a year and a half to get good at it. We only have five sessions for throwing, and then one for glazing (which doesn't interest this blind person). While "quitter" is a dirty word for me, I'm not having fun. It's a waste of money to quit, but is it better to make yourself miserable just to get your money's worth? So I crafted this "I quit" e-mail and will sleep on it.

> I need to drop Ceramics. For me to be successful, I've discovered I need an aide or coach. I appreciate your showing me what to do, but then I end up doing it wrong more times than right. I'm practicing bad habits. If you ever become aware of an art student who'd like to do service learning by serving as a coach, I'd like to try it again. Thanks for trying.

> Kathie

After thinking about it overnight, I felt brave enough to ask for what I needed instead of just slinking away. I sent the following e-mail instead.

I need to do something different in Ceramics. For me to be successful, I've discovered I need an aide or coach. I appreciate your showing me what to do, but then I end up doing it wrong more times than right. I'm practicing bad habits. If by magic, you were aware of an art student who'd like to do service learning serving as a coach, I'd like to try it. If one can't be found in four days, could Continuing Education give me a voucher to take the class again when we've been able to have an aide in place from day one? Thanks for your help in figuring out a good solution for this problem.
Kathie

June 15: Resurrection

"I don't care if you're dead. Jesus is here and he wants to resurrect somebody"—Rumi

With the stress of finding a home for Fran gone and the stress of figuring out what to do about Ceramics gone, I'm beginning to feel like someone is pumping helium into my very deflated balloon. Again I notice that the birds are singing, the sun is shining and I can say "good morning" to people on the street.

June 16: Bloomsday

Bloomsday commemorates the day on which the events of James Joyce's novel *Ulysses* took place. Joyce chose June 16, 1904, for the setting because it was the day of his first date with his future wife.

The first modern celebration of Bloomsday occurred in the early 1950s. Joyce dealt with vision issues most of his adult life and was almost completely blind when he died. Because of this, blindness organizations are starting to hold fundraisers and educational workshops about alternate formats for reading, in conjunction with Bloomsday celebrations.

In the back of my mind, I hope to read *Ulysses* and other classics that I missed in college sometime during retirement. I'm beginning to wonder if retirement will be long enough. As long as my favorite thriller authors keep publishing at least a book per year, probably not.

June 17: So Many Books, So Little Time

I'm always looking for new books, from Bookshare, to *The New York Times Book Review*, to National Public Radio's book section. Today's haul included these titles: *The Tao of Bridge, How to Light a Fart, Vegan Junk Food, I Used to Miss Him, But My Aim Is Improving*, and *Jesus Rode a Donkey*. I don't know if I'll ever read any of them, but the titles made me smile. Every day the list gets longer.

I'm reading *A Land More Kind Than Home* by Wiley Cash. I downloaded a poem by the new poet laureate. I also came upon a review, by Jane Juska, of *What to Look for in Winter: A Memoir in Blindness* by Candia McWilliam

I sent the following e-mail to a Disability Studies in the Humanities LISTSERV I'm on. "In her June 17 *San Francisco Chronicle* review, Ms. Juska wrote that for a reader or a writer, blindness is the worst thing that can happen. Any of you writers out there willing to call her on this?"

Not getting much response, I sent the following to the Books editor of the *San Francisco Chronicle*. It wasn't great, but somebody needed to say something.

"I'm writing in response to Ms. Juska's review of *What to Look for in Winter: A Memoir in Blindness* by Candia McWilliam. I strongly disagree with Ms. Juska's statement.

Worse things can befall a person, but for a reader and a writer, blindness tops the list. Even before technology provided us with talking computers, and organizations like Bookshare that has 140,000 downloadable books for blind and visually-impaired people, there were writers like Milton, Thurber and James Joyce who were visually-impaired.

Since Joyce dealt with vision issues most of his adult life, and was almost completely blind when he died, it is particularly ironic that your review appears on the day after Bloomsday. I'm blind from birth and agree that it is undeniably more difficult to find desired books in alternate formats. The only braille book I had in college or graduate school was a calculus text. But I did get the reading done, as do thousands of blind and visually-impaired people. As people age and some develop visual impairments and blindness, they need to know that the pleasures of reading and writing can most definitely still be theirs."

June 18: When Death Happens

As I get older, I have more friends die and I think more about death. It's not morbid, just a part of life—another event that I don't look forward to, but I know will happen.

Today a friend and I did a role-play for the local hospital that wanted to improve their organ procurement program. It is apparently one of the better ones in the state. They had us role-play twice, once with a doctor, nurse, and chaplain, and then once with just the nurse and chaplain. The family member we were discussing in the role-play was brain-dead. Apparently in Catholic teaching, that "counts" as dead even though the heart might beat. One of the last tests the doctors do is an apnea test to see if the person will breathe if the vent is turned off. If not, that is the time for staff to approach the family for donating organs, tissues, skin (for burn patients), and bones.

As we walked out of the hospital after the role-plays, my friend said she'd call her son (about the age of the child in the role-play) and say she loved him. Today I thank God for the gift of life.

June 19: Transability

A LISTSERV I'm on just had a post about being transabled. I didn't know what that word meant, so I went to Transabled.org. I found that it's people who want to be paraplegic, blind, etc., or who feel they are (in their heads), but aren't in reality. Most would consider them to have a severe mental illness, but they don't see it that way. I wonder if we'll ever have people who want to be old and have all the aches and pains of aging.

June 20: Summertime and the Living Is Easy—or Not!

Today's the first day of summer and I'm all for it. Fresh fruits and vegetables, no ice on the ground, T-shirts and Capri pants instead of bundling up with coats, hats and gloves—what's not to like?

On the other hand, organizing meetings and doing projects, which depend on others, are becoming nightmarish. I need to arrange a phone conference, ten days from now. Nobody will respond with whom I should invite. When new laws go into effect on July 1 about audio description of a few television programs a week, I want to be able to check what programs will be described. Answers from people who should know have ranged from, "No, listings won't be marked," to

"Why are you worried; that's not happening until July 1." When I answered the last by saying I'd lived my life by getting prepared ahead of time for things, she acted like that's your problem not mine! A walk helped, but I may need to sit outside and let the heat bake the let's-get-this-done out of me.

June 21: Getting from Giving

A friend was telling me about a three-generation family she met, while volunteering at a local cancer center. The eldest generation woman was there for treatment, and her daughter and granddaughter were there to support her. At the end, they left saying they'd pray for my friend who had shared she was a cancer survivor too. That same day, I screened a woman for an assistance dog loss phone support group. She shared with me about her semi-retired service dog and her younger service dog. They all went to Episcopal Mass and the priest blessed two dog bones along with the bread. Each of them got something when they went up for Communion. Both were sweet stories and good examples of how much more one gets by "helping" others.

June 22: Happy Retirement

Today I was talking to a neighbor who is retired. On the surface he has it all: reasonable health, enough money to live comfortably, family, and hobbies. But he's not enjoying retirement, living in the past, and mulling over choices he's made. I noticed a book *Master Class: Living Longer, Stronger, and Happier.*

But what does it take to actuate someone, like my neighbor, to actually live longer, stronger, and happier? Being a retired psychologist, of course I recommended counseling, but not everybody will take that road. Maybe a serious illness would jolt him into living, but I wouldn't wish that on anybody. A pet? A new grandchild?

June 23: Now That's a Hard Road!

On June 23, 1926, the first lip-reading tournament in America was held in Philadelphia, Pennsylvania.

Since only about thirty percent of what is said is visible, even if the lip-reader is looking directly at the face of the speaker, it's a major guessing game for deaf or hard of hearing people who rely on lip-reading. Group conversations, like most social situations, are even worse.

Henry Kisor titled his book *What's That Pig Outdoors?: A Memoir of Deafness*, in reference to mishearing the question, "What's that big loud noise?"

Rates of hearing impairment rise as we age. Hearing loss leads to frustration for both speakers and listeners. Hearing aids that work with sound systems in meeting rooms, and on telephones, certainly help but are no panacea. I get frustrated when written matter is not made accessible for me, but not being able to hear daily conversations would drive me nuts. I know what it's like to guess what's in my environment. It's tiring. Occasionally there are funny miscommunications, like the title of Kisor's book, but most of the time I'm sure it's just plain hard. Next time I get frustrated when hard of hearing friends' seemingly ignore what I say, or say, "huh?" let me remember I'm only interacting with them for a little while. They live like that 24/7!

June 24: Impatience

I got an impatiens plant today as a thank you for talking at a literacy organization's celebration for students and tutors. I'd talked briefly about my passion for braille literacy in reading, writing, and use in daily life like card playing. After being very impatient about a number of unresolved issues during the week, I asked if I could have two plants. I'll plant them in front of my house and impatiently watch them grow.

I had to find out how they got that name! Of course Wikipedia had the answer: Latin for "impatience." They're also called touch-me-nots because if you touch the ripe seedpods they shoot seeds several feet.

June 25: A Second or Two Can Help

The Minneapolis' *Star Tribune* of June 25, in the Lifestyle section, had an article about hundreds of crosswalks in Minnesota giving a couple more seconds for the "walk" signal on each green light. The article said that this is based on a federal study, which found that pedestrians don't scamper as fast as researchers thought they did. This is good news for a lot of us who are aging, especially when climbing over mountains of snow at the curbs. I hope Wisconsin will follow Minnesota. When I sent it to a local e-democracy forum, one gal with young children chimed in that it would be good for her too.

June 26: Body Image Problems in the Over-Fifty Set

"Body image can affect more than just teens" by Janice Lloyd, in *USA TODAY*, reports on a first-of-its-kind study looking at older women's body images. It reported that eating disorders are common. Sixty-two percent of those surveyed say their weight or shape has damaged their lives. Historically, eating disorder research has focused on teens and young women. But a study last week in the *International Journal of Eating Disorders*, showed thirteen percent of women, ages fifty and older, struggle with the problem—some for the first time in their lives.

Dislike of the aging body is not news. Millions of dollars have been spent for years to prevent or delay sagging, wrinkling, and graying. Today I was at a meeting to plan for Senior Americans Day workshops on the campus of our local university. One of the people who works in the field of aging was excitedly talking about a workshop to help people control their voices so they didn't "sound old." I was too shocked to question her, but I am still wondering what's wrong with sounding old.

It makes me sad to think of all the time, energy, and money that people spend on fighting natural changes. Working to keep the body strong and functional is great in my book, but fighting time and gravity are different.

Save your body-improvement time and energy for fighting frailty. It is characterized by three of the following five characteristics: unintentional weight loss of ten pounds or more in the past year, self-reported exhaustion, weakness measured by grip strength, slow-walking speed, and low physical activity.

June 27: A Varied Day

Retirement has no typical days, but today is a representative day in some ways. I attended a child's music therapy session, and went to lunch with a friend to mock interview her for an upcoming job interview. I took a nap and made a couple of phone calls to friends. I drafted a newsletter article on tips for pet safety during the summer. I read e-mails, skimmed eight newspapers online, and read some reviews of the book we're discussing at the book club tomorrow. Mental, emotional, and social stimulation aplenty. The day was a little short on physical exercise, but otherwise well-rounded. By the time I say my prayers and listen to the news on the BBC, it'll be bedtime. Low stress, enjoyable work, and gathering with friends—what a fine day.

June 28: Reunions: To Go or Not to Go

I've been getting e-mails for over a year about a big reunion of my high school class. I've never gone to one. I was curious enough to get on the e-mail list, but not enough to go.

Julian Barnes, the author of *The Sense of an Ending*, which I just read for a book club, said that "reunions are an overbuilt story of what never was." I remember having very few friends in high school and surviving it, but not enjoying much of it. The people who were active on the e-mail list seemed to have very different and much fonder memories of it. I'm guessing going to the reunion would take me straight back to the angst of high school and to feeling like I didn't fit in then, and don't fit in now.

When I brought it up to a group of people about my age, half had gone to reunions and enjoyed them, and half hadn't gone and didn't want to. Those who enjoyed it liked the reunions nowadays because nobody was proving anything, just enjoying each other's company.

A few years ago, Seeing Eye had a reunion and several hundred grads went. I didn't even feel tempted by that one. I guess I'm consistently one who makes a few close friends, and doesn't need to keep up or catch up with the rest of the group.

June 29: I Love Computers, But…

I love computers for all the access to information and ease of communication they give me. From scanning the headlines of the local paper and catching up with e-mails before my first cup of coffee in the morning, to skimming several regional and national newspapers before I go to bed, I'm plugged in a lot. I could kill the computer, though, when I'm struggling to update programs like my antivirus software and the screen reader quits talking. I usually reboot and that fixes things.

Lots of experts are weighing in on the downside of all this technology. In the book *Alone Together*, psychologist Sherry Turkle explains how digital devices are affecting our communication and relationships. "What is so seductive about texting, about keeping that phone on, about that little red light on the BlackBerry, is you want to know who wants you," she says. She makes a good point; a great e-mail is no substitute for a hug, and a tweet is not the same as a conversation.

Nicholas Carr points out in *The Shallows: What the Internet is Doing to Our Brains* that the printed book serves to focus our attention, promoting deep and creative thought. The Internet encourages the rapid, distracted sampling of small bits of information from many sources. To me, books are tools and the Internet is a tool. I even notice a difference between reading a book in braille, or as a recording. I vastly prefer braille if it's the Bible, poetry, math, or anything else I want to pause and think about. I like recorded books for listening to the beauty of the spoken language, or when I want to race through a thriller. Sometimes I download a book in electronic speech, which can be speeded up a lot more than regular speech on a CD. So many books, so little time.

As people get older and can't see enough to read, more will be joining me in reading by ear. It is a learned skill, especially when you throw in electronic speech. It is an acquired taste. I see many seniors with failing vision just switching to listening to radio and television. They don't even try learning to use talking computers.

June 30: What is She Thinking?

I'd give a lot of money to know what Fran was thinking this afternoon. For the second time in a week, I was in a duet; this time with her.

The first duet this week was with a friend who teaches blind children. We sang "So Long, It's Been Good to Know Yuh" to a departing music therapy student. She had worked with a young blind child. I'd redone the chorus to mention her internship. Since the teacher and I were truly bad in pitch and rhythm, it was memorable mainly for its "heart." The student music therapist was gracious and professional enough to remain smiling throughout.

This afternoon I was bathing Fran. Usually I sing "Showers of Blessing" for bath music, but somehow this time I started singing "Leaning on the Everlasting Arms." Since I only knew one line, there was a lot of repetition. About five minutes in, Fran started singing/humming along. We did a duet for several minutes. When I switched to "Showers of Blessing," she stopped singing.

Did she sing along because she learned the melody and words, and decided to harmonize? Or did she sing along in pain, as in, "If you don't quit, I'll howl?"

☽

July 1: To Your Health!

Trolling through newspapers, I found health articles extolling apple peels, pointing a finger at white rice for causing diabetes, and suggesting that regular salad dressings may help you absorb more of the vegetables' nutrients than low fat dressings. All these findings are important I'm sure, until next week's studies show something different. As a nation of overweight, avid consumers of health information, I think we're nuts!

What makes the most sense to me, living in the Midwest, is moderation and a Mediterranean diet, but with a Midwest twist. I try to eat what's in season. I don't believe in demonizing foods as "bad." That just makes me want them more. I have friends who can't eat just one or two cookies, so maybe they shouldn't eat them at all, but for those of us who can, why not? Food is there to bring nutrition and pleasure.

July 2: New Golden Rule for Women

According to *Oil for Your Lamp*, by Lisa Hammond and BJ Gallagher, there should be a new golden rule for women: do for others as you do for yourself. I was just trying to convince a gal to consider this idea. She works eighty-hour weeks so her kids can go to expensive colleges and not have to work. She's about ready to quit being superwoman, but it's a hard decision to make. Women (especially single moms, women with disabilities, and women working in male-dominated fields) find it very hard not to play superwoman.

I wonder if women retirees in general, and me in particular, might have this issue. When I first retired, I think I was on five boards of directors! Collecting stars in my crown? Maybe. Part of it was out of genuine interest. I'm afraid the see-I'm-still-useful mentality was also there. It's still a struggle to lie in bed and read a book during the day. After I finish supper, and if the day's work is done, it's okay to read for fun. I wonder if I could even do a staycation. Maybe I'll try one on July 4.

July 3: Hope

I did a talk on hope for a small group tonight. It made me think again about my hopes now compared to years ago. Strength for the journey, sense of God's presence, and hope to make the world a little better each day are my current top hopes. These are less specific than my old hopes for a particular job, or a problem to work out in a particular way. Hope means things will make sense in the long run, not that particular good things will happen. Sometimes I still have trouble waiting for the long run to come. For example, when will I hear about going back to Seeing Eye? I know in the back of my mind there is a purpose in this waiting. I hope I figure it out.

July 4: Freedom, Independence and the American Dream
On this day, when the second Continental Congress passed the Declaration of Independence, and Henry David Thoreau started his life at Walden Pond, I think a lot about freedom and independence. I'm deeply grateful for the freedoms I have, including freedom from want, fear, and disease. Then there are the freedoms to vote, to worship, to associate with those I choose to, to work for the common good, and to "pursue happiness," among others. To me, independence more often means interdependence. Even Thoreau had to get his groceries somewhere!

A program on National Public Radio asked what song typified the American Dream. "This Land Is Your Land," by Woody Guthrie, occurred to me. As I volunteer and work for justice in various ways, it feels more and more like "my land."

"We Shall Overcome" also quickly came to mind. Getting no response from either my state representative or senator about tweaking the law to ensure secret ballots for all in Wisconsin, I realized again the necessity of a "we" to overcome. I need the backing of a disability group, the ACLU, or some other big group to get even this tiny change to happen. But since this is a holiday, I'm just going to kick back and celebrate that I have the freedom to try advocating. Celebrating will include a walk with my guide dog, listening to stirring American music on National Public Radio, and laughing at *The Capitol Steps'* Fourth of July political comedy hour.

July 5: Truth Telling and Lying
I read a study that said, on average, we lie once a day. That seems like a lot to me. Now, I'm watching myself like a hawk. I'll fill in on how often I lie when I catch myself; honest!

On the other end of the continuum, I just finished reading *26: a Behind the Scenes Tour of Life with Cerebral Palsy* by Stuart Maloney.

He's a memoirist who tells the truth about the effects of his disability on his family relationships, his dating, and his self-image. The most honest memoirs of aging I've read are
Anna Quindlen's and Barbara Johnson's. *Losing My Mind* by Thomas Debaggio is an unrivaled self-portrait by a man with the early stages of Alzheimer's disease.

July 6: The Call

The call came today saying I might have a spot in the Seeing Eye class on July 30th and they were wondering if it was convenient for me. Of course I said it was and jumped into several hours of planning and list-making to make sure the pet food program I run and other responsibilities get taken care of for the eighteen days I'll be gone. I told a few friends and one asked if I was excited. I am not; just relieved it's happening and sad that in about three weeks I'll be saying bye to Fran. I'll miss her smart and sweet presence in my life and ache about causing her pain. If she's like my other retired dogs, she'll accept the change and enjoy the new home. There will be a hard couple of days for her when I drop her off with her new mom.

Since the call, Fran has been sticking to me like glue, so I'm sure she caught on to my frenzy of planning. I hope excitement grabs me the day I meet Young and Foolish.

July 7: Reverence for the Written Word

Today I saw a touching reverence for the written word. An eighty-year-old lady had called the Senior Center wishing to dispose of some Braille reading and writing materials. She found them lurking in her basement from forty years ago when her child of ten was fascinated with the Braille code. The Senior Center e-mailed me and I called her to arrange a drop off of the box of materials. Included in the box were 1972 price lists of Braille paper, in Braille. She handed me the box as if it contained Holy Writ. It reminds me of when I throw away a Braille magazine on an airplane or in a hotel room and someone rushes to present it back to me. They wouldn't do this with a print magazine someone had tossed in the trash. Is it because Braille is bulky and expensive or just mysterious? In any case, it's touching to see the written word treated with such reverence.

July 8: Audible Charades

I was trying to design a game that blind and sighted kids and adults could play. I came up with audible charades. I have a bunch of Beanie Babies which I've labeled in Braille. The game will begin with the team of adults turning their backs and the team of kids giving sound and word clues. The first adult to guess the animal gets it for their bag. The goal is to get the most animals captured in your bag. Today, I sent a friend home with Internet homework of figuring out what three Beanie Baby birds are supposed to be. She's come up with Moluccan cockatoo for one so far.

July 9: Blogging

With a student's help, I posted my first blog entry today and sent out a link to a few friends and LISTSERVS. Within an hour someone had commented on it. I'm not sure how many followers I will have, but at least one! I'll have more when I put some kind of widget on it so they can follow by e-mail or RSS, but I need sighted help to do the widget thing.

After I'd bumbled around and done this, I downloaded the book *How to Blog a Book*. Normally, I'm one of those people who never read instructions first. Now I can read how I should do it. I'm thinking I'll post once a week, but we'll see what the experts say.

July 10: Sun Tzu and Aging

A veteran I know who is fighting some discrimination because of his war injuries recommended Sun Tzu's works on warfare to me. It turns out several books have been written applying his teachings to business, women's issues etc. Here are some points to ponder as we age and continue to fight the good fight:

Keep your friends close and your enemies closer; he who wishes to fight must first count the cost; to fight and conquer in all your battles is not supreme excellence; supreme excellence consists in breaking the enemy's resistance without fighting.

July 11: It's Official

I sent out this mass e-mail:

It's official! Fran will retire to her new home in Eau Claire on July 29 and I'll head out to New Jersey on July 30 to get Young

and Foolish. I'll be back in Eau Claire on August 16. While in New Jersey at Seeing Eye I'll have e-mail access, so keep in touch. I hope to have time to let you know what Young and Foolish is and how Fran is doing. I apologize for the mass e-mail. Fran is lying by my feet reminding me to send her best.
Kathie

I got the following wonderful response (among others):

> Congratulations and our best to all three of you! Good dog, Fran! I am totally jealous of your retirement, Girl! Kathie, I hope you find your best dog yet! Young & Foolish, you are a lucky pup! Do good work. You have my sympathy...Kathie is a vegetarian! No stray pork chops in your future!
> Love to you all,
> Sally & Dave

July 12: Thoreau and Staying Human

I learned this, at least, by my experiment; that if one advances confidently in the direction of his dreams, and endeavors to live the life which he has imagined, and he will meet with a success unexpected in common hours.
—Henry David Thoreau, *Walden*

Rick Bragg, in an article in *Southern Living*, talks about "loafering." Tim Kreider recommended slow living, being lazy, and wasting time instead of "busyness."
It's Thoreau's birthday! As he said: "the more slowly trees grow at first, the sounder they are at the core."

As I visited Fran's next home, I sat my hind end on the swing in the backyard and just enjoyed the ambiance for a couple of minutes. Amazing how restful this micro-vacation was!

July 13: Playing Games

A family with preteen and teenage kids came over and it was a great excuse to play games. We played my newly minted game of audible charades. A dice game where one could win dimes and a craft where we made collages were also popular. My American history quiz was a bust except for the over-forty folk. Then in the evening I played bridge. Play to win, play to have fun, play as an excuse for eating and talking—it's all good.

July 14: Stochasticity:

Everything comes to us that belongs to us if we create the capacity to receive it.

—Rabindranath Tagore

National Public Radio had a segment on stochasticity/randomness and how much it rules our lives. But how do we know if something is random? When I was moving to Eau Claire and the perfect house went on the market when I needed it to, was that random or meant to be? When I sit next to a "random" person at Mass and end up becoming friends, was that really random?

Depending on whether it is a good event or not, we may attribute it to fate, God, a Higher Power, luck, or "the committee in charge of messing up my life" that one friend swears by.

July 15: Friends

We are all travelers in the wilderness of this world and the best that we can find in our travels is an honest friend.

—Robert Louis Stevenson

Today friends gave my soon to retire guide dog a gift certificate for a pet food store and homemade duck and potato treats (she's on Natural Balance Duck and Potato formula food because of allergies). Now that we're down to two weeks until retirement, friendly gestures like these really help carry both of us through this hard time.

July 16: Information Access, Seniors and People with Disabilities

The American Library Association has declared today to be information access day. As I limp along in the slow lane of the information superhighway, posting my second blog entry, and downloading more podcasts than I'll ever get to, I glory in what's out there nowadays in accessible information for blind people. Newsline provides access to hundreds of newspapers and magazines, although not my local paper.

The National Library Service and Bookshare provide as many books as would be available in a small town's public library.

As is usual, the glass is both half full and half empty. A friend told me about attending a public lecture with extended family that included two deaf adults. Nothing in the publicity or on the website mentioned how to request an interpreter. Some of the family, including the deaf people, sat in the back and those who could hear texted key phrases from the talk to the Deaf. The usual provisos about turning off your cell phones were in the program. Unfortunately, the speaker announced that even if you were sitting in the back, you had to turn them off, because it was distracting. So they did and the deaf family members didn't get much out of the program.

On another front, two weeks into a federally mandated provision of a few hours a week of described television programming, not much is happening. Even people who live in the top twenty-five markets, where the network says the program is described, are only occasionally reporting they can watch and get description. The cable companies are saying it must be your equipment, or the network, or somebody else.

Everyday things like going to a program with the rest of your family or watching television are not easy. Even with laws, technology, and people of good will, we're lucky if it happens at all. People just joining the disability club as they age have a hard time understanding this. Yes, access should be there, but often it just isn't. So I e-mail asking how to get access, follow up when I don't hear back, and enjoy what is there. One thing I enjoy is the link a friend sent me that took me to a business selling funny signs (which I adore reading and can read online).

July 17: Truth and Certainty

As I age, I am certain of less and less and really don't often think I have a corner on the truth. I was reminded of this as I prepared to lead a discussion in my book club of "American Dervish" by A. Akhter. It's a coming-of-age story of a young Muslim boy in the Midwest. No plot spoiler here I hope, but in his younger years he was sure he knew certain things like marrying out of your faith were just plain wrong. I had never heard that Muslims believe Christ was not crucified and that he will come back before the final judgment day. That isn't my belief, but

I feel no need to start a holy war about it or convert the next Muslim I meet to my beliefs.

I hear that we get more rigid as we age, and sometimes I see that in myself. I wouldn't try and change someone's religious beliefs but politics is a different matter—there I'd like to make converts.

July 18: Stuff

A retired friend and I were talking about how much stuff we've accumulated and why. Both of us are savers of magazines that we mean to go through someday. My only problem is that Braille is much bulkier than print so my stacks look worse than a sighted person's. I've been making a dent in a few stacks because summer is an easier time to recycle than winter. With new dog coming soon I know I won't have time. Why do we save stuff that we'll never use? Parents who grew up in the Depression instilled in their kids the value "waste not, want not." I falsely believe I'll have more time later to do this. Knowledge is precious so I want to hoard it. I can't clean it all at once, so why try! But when I do it a little bit at a time, progress really is made, or at least recycling buckets are filled.

July 19: Happy Music

"Singin' in the Rain" turns sixty today. I'm no big fan of musicals, but the title song is a favorite of mine. Other happy music from musicals I like include: "Whistle a Happy Tune" and "The Hills are Alive" from *The Sound of Music*. In her book *What Would Barbra Do?* Brockes reminisces about her mother who lived her life like it was a musical and always had a song for every occasion. Clearly there are worse ways to go through life than with this kind of happy soundtrack.

July 20: Sculptures

Our town gets a couple of dozen new sculptures each year on display. If a group in town puts together enough money to buy one, then it stays. Otherwise they all move on. Last year there were two stand-outs: one of a boy with a cast on his leg putting a stethoscope on a dog's chest and one called "Circle of Friends" was of a gal reading to book characters. One now lives at the hospital and the other lives near the library. A friend and I took a tour to admire the sculpture by the library and to look at the new crop. My favorite was a sculpture of a shepherd holding a lamb; the texture on the lamb was so well done. There was another of a boy holding up a fish he'd caught that was also interesting because of the tubular construction (sort of like a line drawing but three dimensional). I don't often look for art to enjoy by feel, but it was fun to examine all the different ways the artists used to get their ideas across.

July 21: It's the Little Things I'll Miss

I often notice how smart and sweet Fran is. But she just proved the smart part again this afternoon. We were napping and I got up to use the john and grab a snack downstairs. Since I was only going for a minute I didn't bother to put on my pants. She looked and knew I'd have to come back for my britches so she didn't bother to get up. That is an observant canine.

I'm sure my next dog will do his/her guide work well I'm sure or he/she wouldn't be assigned to me. We wouldn't leave Seeing Eye as a team unless they were sure we were safe. It's the little things I'll miss about Fran; the comfort of a working relationship forged over several years and the many experiences we've shared. The knowing what each other are thinking takes at least six months to happen I think. And it will develop with Young and Foolish. I'm sure I'll tell the new dog about Fran and her wonderful traits, partly to let it out and partly for him/her to know that I do notice and love the little things as well as the job duties of keeping me safe.

As the song we learned in Girl Scouts, said "make new friends but keep the old. One is silver and the other is gold." Once we part, I won't see Fran until she's settled in her new home, but the golden memories will be close at hand in my heart.

July 22: What I Know for Sure after Thirty-nine Years of Being a Guide Dog Handler

As I head off to train with my ninth Seeing Eye dog, I'm sad and in a reflective mood. In a couple of years I will have had a Seeing Eye dog for half the time the Seeing Eye organization has been in existence. That entitles me to be philosophical, right?

The first thing I know for certain is each working dog is a unique gift; no two are alike! Your first dog often changes your life so much that the second dog suffers by comparison. When you realize that of course they're different and that they have different strengths, you can still honor that first dog and go on to fully embrace number two, three, etc. Each dog does their job, but the fun and sometimes frustrating part is to figure out how to work with that individual dog so he/she shines.

Each of my working dogs has shaped my character in different ways. My first dog taught me to be positive instead of crabby when my expectations were not met. My soon-to-be retired dog showed such courage in telling me that she needed to retire. She refused to work when she thought she could not safely do so because of a vision problem. I am in awe of her. Then there are the funny little things they do that show you they definitely do think. For example, I've taught each of my dogs the words "up" and "down" so when we go into a building they'll find the stairs for me. As they reached middle age (about seven) each one started showing me the elevator instead of the stairs.

I've learned from retiring dogs that it's never easy no matter how many times you do it, but you will get through it and you will love again. I grieve the entire process of retiring a dog: the decision, the actual retirement, and eventually the dog's death. Like with any grief, rituals like a retirement party and writing a bio for the family who adopts the dog help. Coaching friends to treat it as seriously as they would a death or divorce may be necessary. A few empathic souls "get it" that working dogs are very different from pets. They do the right things like listening and showing up to help with the transition or just bringing a dish. I'm convinced more would if they realized this dog is my best friend, my eyes, and my key to safe transportation.

I'm still learning from my dogs that you should be joyful in greeting each new day, be quick to love and forgive, enjoy the little things like fresh water and a bowl of food, and that a wagging tail wins a lot of friends. I wonder what I'll learn from Young and Foolish.

July 23: Agley

Today's word for the day was "agley" meaning askew. I thought it was appropriate for my life; Fran's retirement has really knocked my world agley. I felt sorry for myself. Then as so often happens, something pushed me back to my senses. In today's case it was an e-mail about flight 15, one of the thousands of flights that were grounded on September 11, 2001. This flight landed in Canada and the townspeople were so hospitable that the grateful passengers set up a scholarship fund and had a ten year reunion a couple of years ago. Talk about an event knocking people's lives agley. I have my life, my health, my home, my friends, my memories, and a new guide dog waiting for me. I can acknowledge how agley my life is and still count my blessings.

July 24: She Was Younger than Me!
Sally Ride, the first American woman in space died today. She was younger than me! Increasingly I notice people younger than me dying. We all know death will happen, even to us, but this underlines it.

In addition to thinking I'm lucky to be alive, younger people dying makes me think about all those chores I'd better get done soon. Do I really want my heirs to have to toss out thirty year old lecture notes? If I want to change my will, I really should do it now! I'd better do those positive things on my bucket list too. There's always tomorrow is not always a true statement.

July 25: Friends Again
When I count my blessings, I count you twice.
—Irish Proverb

This is a week of really feeling blessed by friends. They've called, taken me out for a meal, stopped by to say "bye" to Fran, e-mailed, and I'm sure many have prayed. When I get stressed I don't want to eat—which is very unusual for me. Someone coming by to share a bite is really helpful. A friend who lives in assisted living gave me advice on how to tolerate people at your table three times a day; just paste a smile on your face. Others step up to water the flowers and take in the mail. Of course watering also includes picking the tomatoes! Fran is sticking very close and being a physical presence as well as doing what guiding she can. My friends and their acts of friendship really do count twice or more this week.

July 26: 22nd Anniversary of the Americans with Disabilities Act
The Americans with Disabilities Act (ADA) is twenty-two today. I'll celebrate because some things are better for both blind people and for people with other disabilities. Some of the improvements that have benefited me as a blind person include: requiring public entities like boards I'm on, and Social Security to provide information in

Braille or other accessible formats, standardized guide dog access instead of differing laws in every state, and backing from the ADA to do describer training for library staff.

Changes other blind people noted include: ability to pick from four movie theaters in my area which have audio description; use of accessible iPhone and Android systems; the Lite Rail in the area has talking ticket machines, use of talking ATMs; Braille signage in public taxis showing the driver number if a report needs to be filed; automated announcers in busses that announce the stop as the bus stops; accessible street crossings with audible pedestrian signals.

My hope is that as more people age into the disability club, accessibilities will keep improving for all. Half the people over sixty-five have disabilities; it only makes sense to build with universal design and think about access for all in services and programs. I'll celebrate by reading newspapers online with my screen reader and by downloading an accessible copy of a new thriller from Bookshare.

July 27: Older Women in Novels

To get my mind off life as I know it I enjoy reading books. I read the *Red Hat Society: Acting Their Age* by Regina Hale. It's a cute little novel where older women are smart, perky, and wise. Nancy Thayer has written several *Hot Flash Club* novels. In them, four women realize that the time has come to use it or lose it. As the book jackets say: "they realize that they can have it all, perhaps for the first time in their lives. And though what sags may never rise again, feeling sexy has no expiration date—and best of all, with a little help from her friends, a woman can always start over . . . and never, ever, give up what matters most. Girlfriends forever!" Rita Lakin's detective series *Getting Old Is Criminal* features retired ladies solving murders. All these books are cute and fun but not much more than HenLit (if that's the older ladies' version of chick lit).

For more literary, but still good reads with older characters I like *The Best Exotic Marigold Hotel* and *Crossing to Safety.* The characters have depth and charm and do some thinking. It's great to be able to read about people older than me and see what's to come.

July 28: Olympics and Non-Olympic Sports that Should Be

A legally blind South Korean archer set the first Olympic world record!

A combined hearing and deaf choir did the British National anthem in the opening ceremonies of the 2012 Olympics.

I'd like to imagine some non-Olympic contests that we could have in the aging Olympics. They would include: remembering the name of your child's first dentist when you meet him/her in the grocery store; the time in minutes you can refrain from saying "I told you so" when your adult child discovers a truism (like you need to consider health insurance when looking for a job), the number of grocery items you can recall when your list blows away in the parking lot, and how graceful a recovery you can make when your false teeth fall out at dinner.

July 29: Last Church and Fran's Last Day of Work

We read Scripture today so we got to march out of church first. Fran likes doing that and it seems appropriate that we did it today to celebrate what a gift from God she is. She also got to lick a little kid who adores her and vice versa. It was a good ending for her church work.

Thanks to all my friends' kinds' help throughout the process. We dropped Fran off at supper time with a fine dowry. Rae was ready to welcome her. I think they will become good friends quickly. I'll miss the little weasel a lot but I know she's in good hands. Tomorrow it's off to New Jersey to begin a new relationship. I thanked my friends and asked them to keep me updated on life in the real world.

Writing this brings tears to my eyes. It's a gut wrenching experience to retire a dog even though I've done it seven times now. I'm blessed that I have friends who will drive me to and from the new home, provide food afterwards, and sit and eat with me. They remind me by their presence that I'm part of a caring community and am not alone in my grief.

July 30: The Secret of Life

Every day has a different secret of life embedded in it for each of us, but today's secret for me was clear: you can do things that you think you can't. I did make it through the day without my heart breaking and I did accomplish what I needed to. Thank goodness for that autopilot in each of us that just motors onward through the muck of life. There were tears, but not a lot. Somehow when I'm really hurting, the tears go inward. A favorite Hemingway quote sums up the day: "Life breaks us all but in the end we are stronger in the broken places". I hope I will be.

July 31: Journeying

St. John of the Cross wrote, "If a man wants to be sure of the road he treads on, he must close his eyes and walk in the dark." I felt very much like my eyes were closed as I flew to New Jersey without a dog by my side. Airline helpers took me to the wrong gate so I missed my connecting flight; I'm not sure if their eyes were closed, too!

Seeing Eye is the oldest guide dog school in the United States, and I've been going there for almost half of its existence. It used to have mostly ex-military dog handlers as instructors and was much more formal and hierarchal than it is now. However its core values of respect for the individual and humane training of dogs for guide work have not changed. Other students ranged in age from twenty- to seventy-year-olds and were from all over the United States and Canada. Each individual pays a nominal fee, although the actual dog-human team costs $65,000 to produce. Initially, students walk with their instructor and discuss any preferences of breed or special life circumstances that might influence a good match. I'm a bit slower than when I was younger but I still need a dog good in public to accompany me from meetings, to visiting nursing homes, to guest lecturing in elementary and college classrooms. My instructor was half my age, but I sensed some good maturity and dedication to her work even through my fog of grief. The schedule (up at 5:30 a.m. and not done with lectures and walks until 8:30 p.m.) and the stress of transitions makes this far from a vacation. Staff are kind and competent, but it's not home. A necessary journey has begun.

☽

August 1: New Beginnings

And suddenly you know: It's time to start something new and trust the magic of beginnings.
—Meister Eckhart

A day and a half after arriving; I was matched with Luna, a fifty-one-pound yellow Labrador. Luna was raised by a couple with a twenty-one-year-old daughter who had raised several other Seeing Eye dogs. To me, it is always a miracle that caring individuals will pour enormous amounts of care and love into a dog for a year and then say "goodbye" and "good luck" to the dog, as it goes into months of training to become a guide dog.

Luna's first placement was a home training for a blind gal with a young child. Unfortunately, the gal had medical issues and had to stop training within a week. Luna went back to Seeing Eye for more training with a new instructor and was picked for me. My initial impression was that she was relatively calm and would settle in well. She seemed to be reserving judgment on me and showing me just a little of who she really was. The friendship started tentatively on both our parts.

August 2: Luna Gets a Traffic Check

By the time we'd had the dogs a day, one person had left training (without a dog), and we'd had a traffic check. About twenty years ago, Seeing Eye started having instructors drive cars and cut in front of working teams to be sure handlers and dogs stopped quickly and/or backed up out of harm's way. They did this because distracted drivers often do not obey the law and stop when a blind person with a dog or cane is crossing the street. They have intensified this every time I've been here, which must mean drivers are getting worse. In any case, Luna and I stopped just fine. But then Luna did something I've never seen a dog do. After we were out of the street, she turned around and gave the staff member who was driving a really dirty look as he came out of the parking lot. If she could have raised one finger, she would have. Both the staff driver and my trainer were hooting with laughter as I got her turned around and moving forward. Apparently this little girl dog has spirit!

August 3: Finding Humor

After all scheduled activities, meetings, meals, taking the dogs out to potty four times per day, etc. were completed, a few of us were in the lounge talking and trying to figure out a game we could all play. I explained audible charades, which I had made up for a blind child I know, where you make noises or give word clues for what you're thinking of. One person made a rude noise in derision, somebody else guessed "the bean soup we had for lunch" and it went downhill from there. Everybody was laughing until they cried. Much stress was relieved. We went on to play a different game mind puzzles (not in Braille so an instructor read them). Bean soup had served another purpose than nourishment today.

August 4: Luna really Works!

Today, we went on a path around the grounds called the leisure path that students are encouraged to walk without instructor supervision. The first walk without an instructor must be like the first time a kid gets to drive the car without a parent riding along. You know that the dogs are trained to work but you always wonder, will they work for me? When I go home and there's no instructor around, what will happen? The leisure path is a safe place to try it out. Luna worked! It was not perfect. We're still learning to dance together and read each other's moves, but we made it around the path!

August 5: Vegetarianism

I read an article today that reported five percent of Americans are vegetarian. I've been vegetarian for about forty years now and have enjoyed the increasing availability of vegetarian food. The first time I came to Seeing Eye, their idea of vegetarian meals was giving me more fruits and vegetables. Finally, when I was having trouble with diarrhea, I asked them to just give me an egg, a glass of milk, or a small piece of cheese instead of the meat course of the meal, and that worked better. This time they've had several meat substitutes (some better than others) and some wonderful little vegetable rolls. If I ever end up in a nursing home, I wonder if vegetarian food worth having will be an option.

August 6: Clever Birds

I love to read about how clever birds are. Crows and ravens use tools; the males steal the tools from the females. They recognize people they don't like years later. . Today, I heard a new one. Traffic lights at some intersections have audible signals installed. The first ones, twenty years ago were different tweets and chirps to indicate which way was clear to cross. Now, they have an electronic voice saying "clear to cross South Street" instead because mocking birds were imitating the tweets. Damn clever birds!

August 7: Eternity and Living in Community
Eternity is not something that begins after you are dead. It is going on all the
time.
—Charlotte Perkins Gilman

Living in the classroom of twenty people, under stressful conditions began to feel like an eternity. Cliques are developing and people,
not dogs, are beginning to snap and growl. It's only for eighteen days if
you're a veteran or twenty-five days if you're a first timer, but it feels like
forever. Each interaction when I have to decide whether to take offense,
make a joke, say something kind (or not) is a battle. I've established my
sanity spots (a bench outside and a computer work station in the basement). It's a special struggle to share "my places" with someone else who
rightly believes they are there for all to use. One day at a time has
become my litany.

August 8: Technology Strikes Again
Many of the students here have iPhones and some have Siri, the
talking app that you can ask questions of, like what's the weather forecast, or where's the closest Burger King? After a lecture on dog health
care, a student asked Siri where to get dental wipes. They're similar to
baby wipes except they are used for wiping dogs' teeth. Siri thought she
heard "genital wipes" and was readying an answer when the student
turned her off to the hoots and hollers of all riding in the van to the
training center in town. We never did find out if she could find dental
wipes.

August 9: Nurturing Self-Esteem of Others
As the second-oldest student in this month's class at Seeing Eye,
I felt a calling to try to help others when I could. Often, it has involved
sharing my experiences, not advice as much as what I've learned. Today,
the discussion was a group grumble about how much they hated being
blind and how there was nothing good about it. These people were in
their twenties and thirties and are looking at a long life ahead of them.
It really made me sad to hear them talk that way. I don't deny at all that
there are many frustrations to being blind, but if there weren't the good
parts, why get up in the morning? One of the grumblers is book smart

and loves to argue. I bet her a quarter that she couldn't think of a good part of blindness. If she could come up with an example by lunch, I would owe her a quarter. She took the challenge and by lunch had two, so I had to pay up. She thought of having a guide dog and getting to take her dog with her everywhere. A good use of fifty cents I hope.

August 10: Stress Management, Planned and Spontaneous

Because the situations we are encountering with our dogs are getting more complicated, we had a lecture and demonstration on dog massage in the evening. During the day, we rode escalators, elevators, buses, and trains. The dogs had done them in training, but not while guiding a blind person. Luna did very well, but I'm sure it was stressful. We were all spread out in a recreation room sitting by our dogs ready to massage them. I'd been placed next to a corner where there was a stuffed, life-sized toy dog with a harness. Luna took the massage time to squirrel around trying to bite that dog's tail, roll on her back, and do everything but get massaged. To me, she was managing her stress her way so I didn't force an official massage on her. Watching her goof around relaxed me, so all was good.

August 11: Balancing Act

As I respond to e-mails and start making arrangements for get-togethers and meetings when I return to Eau Claire, I feel like I'm balancing between two worlds. The world of Seeing Eye with rules (nobody pets your dog, you don't tell people the dog's name, etc.) versus the real world where sometimes letting the dog be petted and saying, "Her name is Luna" works better than saying "I can't tell you." There are reasons for the rules and simply going with them is easier than making decisions as situations present themselves. Soon I will reenter the real world where my new Seeing Eye dog will be of momentary interest to many, but focusing on her adjustment will be just part of my reality. Maybe it's like getting out of the hospital or returning from military service. This life experience you've been through is profound for you but of limited interest to others. I guess that's why some join LISTSERVs of guide dog handlers. Going to a coffee shop as a group and listening to people at other tables reminded me there is a world out there and ready or not, I'll be back in it in a week.

August 12: Saying Thanks to Puppy-Raisers

Today, I found out about Luna's puppy-raising family and wrote them a thank-you note. Because of Seeing Eye rules, it had to be anonymous, but I tried hard to make them know it was heartfelt. I wrote:

Dear Luna's Family,

Thank you from the bottom of my heart for raising Luna. I am a middle-aged person living in the Midwest who is active in my community. All those hours you put into perfecting Luna's social skills in a variety of situations will really come in handy as I give talks, attend meetings and go to church. I love to walk on a nature trail so she'll still get to spend time outdoors. I have friends with cats and dogs so she'll get to have four-legged friends as we get settled in back home. I can already tell she's smart and sweet, and I love her dearly. Thank you and God bless you for raising her and the others you have raised. Your work changes lives.

Gratefully yours,
Luna's new person

August 13: Trust and Trotting

Luna and I have a fairly slow walking pace, ideal for hot, muggy, New Jersey August days, construction zones, and Eau Claire winters. But when the weather's cool and I'm sure of my footing, it would be fun to trot. We're experimenting with trotting down a long hall at Seeing Eye. She definitely can, and I think we both enjoy it. But when you're just learning to dance together, it sure is easier to waltz than to rumba!

August 14: Luna the Flirt

Today, I had my exit interview with the president of Seeing Eye. I had several ideas for him, particularly about graduates taking more active roles in fundraising. It's hard to tell if anything will come of them. He said that many graduates don't want to have anything to do with fundraising or contributing; they just want to take and not give back. I know Luna had an impact, anyway. His male Labrador snuck out of his bed in the office and came over to sniff her. I'll bet anything she batted her cute, blond eyelashes.

August 15: Farewells

Seeing Eye discourages giving instructors gifts. I wrote a little doggerel on behalf of my small group, and we gave it to the instructor when we went out to an ice cream parlor. I wanted to fuss over the instructor, compliment her, and reminisce but my fellow students did not, so we didn't. I guess everybody does farewells differently. I leave cautiously optimistic about Luna's and my teamwork, very grateful for the training, and glad to return to my own home and routines.

August 16: Letting Go

Letting go of control is hard for me. Maybe it's because I'm an adult child, or maybe it's because I'm blind and need to advocate often. In any case, it's sure true. As I dealt with negotiating to switch flights home because the delay we had would mean a missed flight and arriving home eight hours late, I could do it calmly instead of angrily. Letting go of being as fast a walker as I was forty years ago and asking for a slower dog was hard. I had to give myself a pep talk or two that slowing down doesn't mean being incompetent. It just means slowing down. It helped to remember my goal of being a member of the fifty-year club, not of winning a race today.

August 17: Difficult Conversations

If you look at every human being as a Divine mirror, you will know yourself and understand life.
—Sherif Baba

Recently, I've had two difficult conversations with friends. In both cases, my disability interacted with theirs, and we needed to figure out how we could coexist without hurting each other. In one case, a friend with a mental illness wanted to say something really inappropriate to someone else in front of me. Since she told me about it before saying it, I said I wasn't comfortable with it. She told me then that I didn't have to listen. Luckily the person walked away before my friend got the chance to say it, so my need for politeness was not trod on. In the other situation, a friend with many disabilities who is becoming frail offered to help me run errands. I was so concerned about her frailty that I couldn't accept, and her feelings were getting hurt. Finally, I asked her what kind of errands would work best for her. It's hard to talk about limits caused by disabilities, especially new ones or invisible ones. But a good friendship is based on honesty, so I'll keep working on it.

August 18: Beautiful Things
When we come upon beautiful things . . . they act like small tears in the surface of the world that pull us through to some vaster space.
—Elaine Scarry

People have been stopping by with food in hand to meet Luna. One gal brought a huge, beautiful eggplant from her garden and it just overwhelmed me. I was home, among people who cared about me and had missed me, and they were sharing their best with me. All that from an eggplant!

August 19: Time Flies
Jim Harrison's excellent poem "Debtors" starts with the lines:

They used to say we're living on borrowed
time but even when young I wondered
who loaned it to us?"

Today was one of those days where I asked myself, "Where did the time go?" I can claim no major accomplishments, but it was a productive and pleasant day. In the Catholic church, between big liturgical seasons like Advent and Lent, it's called "Ordinary time." Most of life is "Ordinary time", and I need to savor days that are ordinary because we do live on borrowed time, and this day will soon be gone.

August 20: An Uncomfortable but Necessary Conversation is Looming
A lot of friends my age are nearing the end of their lives. I'm close enough to them that I want to know their end-of-life wishes, but even with my counseling background, I am very uneasy about bringing up the subject. Ellen Goodman started a website, www.theconversationproject.org, with helpful resources for this conversation. Some of the statistics I found on the website are startling:

Sixty percent of people say that making sure their family is not burdened by tough decisions is "extremely important" but fifty-six percent have not communicated their end-of-life wishes Source: Survey of Californians by the California HealthCare Foundation (2012)

Seventy percent of people say they prefer to die at home but seventy percent die in a hospital, nursing home, or long-term care facility Source: Centers for Disease Control (2005)

Eighty percent of people say that if seriously ill, they would want to talk to their doctor about end-of-life care, but only seven percent report having had an end-of-life conversation with their doctor. Source: Survey of Californians by the California HealthCare Foundation (2012)

Another effort that interests me is a book by Will Schwalbe, *The End of Your Life Book Club*. He describes a book club created by him and his mom, who was dying of pancreatic cancer. The books they shared allowed them to speak honestly and thoughtfully, to get to know each other, ask big questions, and talk about death. Some of the books like *A Year of Magical Thinking* were predictable but some were not like *Girl with the Dragon Tattoo*. I keep reading more and looking for more resources, basically hoping somehow that the perfect opportunity to raise questions will occur.

August 21: Laughing at Ourselves
Phylis Diller died. To me, she was a great comedian because she laughed at herself and helped me laugh at myself, too. As Diller said, "A smile is a curve that sets everything straight." I was describing a situation today to a friend when my guide dog had brushed me up against something, and I'd said "excuse me" before discovering it was a post. After I realized what I'd done, I quickly listened to figure out if anybody was close enough to have heard me. I didn't think so, so I just walked on with a big grin on my face. Otherwise, I probably would have pretended I was talking to the dog.
Recently Betty White was roasted at the Friars' Club, and the *New York Times* headlined the article "Older than the Jokes at Her

Roast." One comedian pointed out that it was a luncheon because they didn't think she'd be awake in the evening. I resemble that remark! My favorite "getting older" joke is one where the minister is visiting an elder and asks them, "Do you ever think about the hereafter?" and the oldster says, "Yes, every time I come into a room I say 'what am I here after?'"

If I run out of things to laugh at, I'm going to download *You're Never too Old to Laugh by* Ed Fischer. Long live laughter.

August 22: We are a Niche Market

I'm so happy to read of the box office success of *The Best Exotic Marigold Hotel.* Two actresses in their late seventies are stars! There's plenty of talk and not reliant on special effects. Maybe I'll even go to see it!

It makes me happy when businesses like Searchlight Pictures offer to older adults something more than Depends and denture cream. *New York Times* large print, *Weekly,* and Doubleday Large print Book Club are good examples. Nasco, which started with educational materials for children, now has a seniors' catalog. With Boomers joining the senior set, I'll bet there will be more products and services coming our way.

August 23: One Week after Coming Home

I wrote my instructor at Seeing Eye:

By tomorrow we will have been home a week and your first time students will be home. Congratulations on finishing another class. Hope your time off is good and most of your moving boxes get unpacked, anyway.

Luna and I are doing great. We do a new route every day, and she is learning them very well. There is a lot of construction on campus, half a block from where I live so she is learning to cross streets in front of big concrete trucks, etc. She's been to the bank, Mass, and the main campus building. She's entertained groups ranging from the bridge group (four hours of lying quietly or sleeping, with a potty break, of course) to a mom and two preschool kids who were afraid of dogs but waved bye to her when they left. She's supervised my watering the garden and my cooking and baking. Her house manners are impeccable.

She's initiated some playing which I take as a very good sign. Eating, sleeping, and pottying are fine. Today, we had a bit of a fight and she tested me by walking past our house when I told her to go home. We're settling in!

August 24: IDisorder and Seniors

I'm reading *IDisorder* by L. Rosen. By 2015, he says eighty percent of the world's population will have a smart phone, tablet or laptop. Sixty-five percent of people in the developed world have two of these. Our dependence on technology has gone beyond convenience into a dehumanizing obsession that permeates society. Social avoidance, attention deficit disorder and   obsessive concern with looks can be some of the downsides of this 24/7 connectivity. Giles Slade in his book *The Big Disconnect* looks at loneliness that may accompany our passion for technology.

Having recently returned from Seeing Eye where I had reduced connectivity, I know the pull to be connected is strong. When you don't reply to an e-mail within twelve hours, people ask if you're ill. As a blind person who has struggled for access, taking breaks from it like Dr. Rosen recommends doesn't make sense. I guess each of us sets limits; I don't tweet but do a little Facebook and a little blogging.

Luckily, I have a dog that makes me take walks, giving me exercise, exposure to nature, and time to let my mind wander. I'm amazed how ideas and solutions to problems pop up on these walks. Rosen's idea of a waiting period of at least five minutes before replying to a personal e-mail makes a lot of sense. I wonder how many of the people who flamed me a few months ago for revealing a piece of the plot in a book review online without announcing "spoiler alert" first waited five minutes to respond. I wonder how to get some of my young friends to prioritize face-to-face interactions over texting. It seems crass to say "talk to me now and text later" in a social situation, but it may be needed. Note to self: read *Would It Kill You to Stop Doing That?* Maybe it'll tell me how to say it.

August 25: Stepping Out in Faith

Faith is the courageous confidence that trusts in the Source of all gifts.
——David Steindl-Rast

Today I got ready to literally step out in faith. I usually sit in the back row at church with several friends. We all consider ourselves to be back-row people — Cafeteria Catholics as some derisively call those of us who use our own consciences to decide right and wrong as opposed to taking our marching orders from Rome. Anyway, the only one of the back-row bunch who was present was a wheelchair user who has communion brought to her. I usually take someone's elbow up to communion so my guide dog won't cut ahead in line, and won't trot right out the door when we return from communion. When we passed the peace I asked the gal sitting in front of me if I could take her elbow. "No" she said because she was giving communion. So I told the wheelchair user that she needed to say "go" when it was time and say "stop" when we came back so we didn't leave before Mass was over. This was only Luna's second trip to Mass so I wasn't really sure how it would all work out. Somehow, I just had a feeling that whatever happened, everything would be okay. Just as I rose up to step out in faith, along came a regular who asked if I wanted to take his elbow. I was right, the community reached out and all was well.

August 26: Weary
Come to me, all you that are weary and are carrying heavy burdens and I will give you rest.
—Matthew 11:28

The last few days I've just been weary. I'm guessing it's trying to catch up on what I've missed while I was away at Seeing Eye, and now orienting Luna to her new surroundings. At first I tried to kick myself into being energetic, but quickly realized it wasn't working. Today I tried to do only what I had to do, and savor the little joys. A friend, who'd walked with Luna and me a week ago, took another walk with us today. She said we were dancing together much better. Other friends and I went out to a lovely little 1950s kind of place. We sat in a gazebo and ate ice cream with the sounds of sprinklers, birds, and cicadas around us. Resting in the good things the Lord provides helps a lot more than kicking yourself!

August 27: Little Things
Make visible what, without you, might perhaps never have been seen.
—Robert Bresson

Today I read two blogs and one well-thought-out letter that is widely distributed to various disability communities. Each of them articulately commented on a disability issue: one possible cut to a service, another lay-off of a worker, and the third people with disabilities having similar dreams to the non-disabled. All of them highlighted concerns for others' needs, not just the writer's. Impressive! Sometimes I get discouraged and think people with disabilities are so weighed down with their own struggles that most don't think of others. These three examples in one day showed the opposite. It reminds me of the last time I visited a friend in assisted living, and she chatted on about what she and others were doing to welcome new residents, and welcomed someone new to her table instead of dwelling on the table mate who had died. We all can bloom where we're planted.

August 28: Showing Up for a Friend's Father's Funeral
Rings and jewels are not gifts, but apologies for gifts. The only true gift is a portion of thyself.
—Ralph Waldo Emerson

Love is what carries you, for it is always there, even in the dark, or most in the dark, but shining out at times like gold stitches in a piece of embroidery.
—Wendell Berry

The small country church was overflowing with family, friends, and neighbors of a good man who had lived ninety years in the same house. Simple hymns were sung to piano accompaniment and after the service we walked down the road to the cemetery. Thirteen tractors were parked on the side of the road, some polished and some clearly pausing their work to be part of a silent parade honoring their neighbor and friend. Church ladies circulated at the luncheon with plates of bars. A community showered love on the family of the departed by showing up and sharing. If there is light in the darkness of grief, it is the love this community showed.

August 29: Luna Joins the Red Hats
At a picnic in the park, Luna was voted into my Red Hat group as a pink scarf member (for those under fifty). She believes in fun and friendship so I'm sure she will make a fine member. After dinner, we played a silly dice game. The woman next to me patronized me, by talking all evening about my dice, which have raised dots, to others at the table.

She then insisted I take half her winnings, since I hadn't won at all. I wasn't going to lose any sleep over losing a dice game. When she said buy something for Luna, I decided to be gracious and take her money. In my younger days I would have set her straight and I still yearn to do it. For her to go from talking *about* me to talking *to* me was a big movement on her part and I needed to be affirming of that. If I can bend my stiff neck enough to get to know her and hear her story, I may end up liking her, but that's a big if at the moment.

August 30: Eternal Perspective on Relationships with People
I shall tell you a great secret, my friend. Do not wait for the last judgment, it takes place every day
—Albert Camus

I am trying to focus on how I treat others today with the perspective of Albert Camus. If these were the last conversations I had with them, what would I be leaving them with? I'm taking that extra ten seconds to thank, encourage, and share an idea.

August 31: Paralympics and Art Exhibits
The 2012 London Paralympic Games marked the fourteenth edition of the Games. They were the largest Paralympic Games in history with an estimated 4,200 participating athletes from 165 countries. Team USA finished with ninety-eight medals (thirty-one gold, twenty-nine silver, and thirty-eight bronze). Congratulations to all of our 227 athletes.

An art exhibit in London opening at the same time as the Paralympics showcases artificial limbs, some of which were decorated to represent the personalities of their former wearers. Imagine what could be done with old walkers, canes, and wheelchairs. Obviously the people who made art from their own old limbs were very comfortable with their prostheses and had a rich relationship with them. When I used to use a long cane, I remember affectionately touching the slight bends in it and thinking about what I encountered that gave it that bend. It took many years for me to go from shame to pride in this mobility device, but it was a good transformation. I'll bet this art exhibit will help some think more positively about their assistive devices.

☽

September 1: Nailed!

Have you learned lessons only of those who admired you, and were tender with you, and stood aside for you? Have you not learned great lessons from those who braced themselves against you, and disputed the passage with you?
—Walt Whitman

It happens more often than it should by chance. I settled in to listen to the homily at Mass this evening and it nailed me exactly. The homily was based on chapter seven of Mark and was about determining what was big stuff versus little stuff, and concentrating on the big stuff. Scribes and Pharisees wanted to debate about cleansing pots and washing hands before you eat. Jesus talked instead about what's in your heart being more important. I was still fussing in my heart about how to address that woman who had patronized me at the Red Hat dice game. Was I Christian to her? Heck no! I barely restrained myself from punching her out. Did I thank her for her charitable impulse and redirect it? Heck no! I was too busy saying, "Don't you dare look down on me." For this scripture and this homily to just happen to hit me three days later, ouch! I get it! Enough already!

On the other hand, on this day in 1904, Helen Keller graduated from Radcliffe, the first deaf-blind person to graduate from college. Now that's big stuff!

September 2: *Winter Journal* and Mortality Thoughts

Paul Auster's second memoir *Winter Journal* and Christopher Hitchens' *Mortality* both concern themselves with the last phase of life. In *Winter Journal* a memoir, Paul Auster quotes a line from Joseph Joubert, the French writer whose work he has translated. "One must die lovable (if one can)."

"We are all going there," Auster writes, "... the question is to what degree a person can remain human while hanging on in a state of helplessness and degradation." I guess the only way to be lovable *then* is to concentrate on being lovable *now*. I'm least gracious when I feel out of control. From the deaths I've observed, that will be a big problem for me. A young girl I know who is dying is quite the opposite. She laughs when others laugh and answers "good" when anyone asks her how she is. It's hard for me to fathom that she knows she's dying, but maybe her trust is so great that she does know and realizes it is good. .

Hitchens says he "must take absolute care not to be self-pitying or self-centered." He takes great pains to face death head on with no self-pity, no reliance on God. Friendships were very important in his life. In his memoir you can tell he hates to leave his world and his friends. His book of essays about "his year of living dyingly" is a compelling memoir. Just like everybody lives differently, everybody dies differently. Auster, Hitchens, and my young friend give three great models.

September 3: Good Work

On Labor Day I thought about the work I did today and thanked God for good work to do. I called twenty or so recipients of our program to provide pet food for seniors and people with disabilities program to catch up on their news and see what they need. One new gal told me about her amazing life of people taking advantage of her, including dumping animals on her to care for. We agreed that we both loved animals (including crows) and that she was a storyteller even though she didn't have any Irish in her.

I tried for a couple of hours to download antivirus software to my laptop, but just couldn't get it done. I'd get close, but the last choice would be not readable by my screen reader. I finally had to quit until I had sighted help. Sometimes completing a job takes help. Luna and I walked to and from a campus building that she'd been to only once without any problem. I don't know how much internal pride she has in her work as of yet, but she was wagging her whole back end by the time I was done praising her.

Now it's time to enjoy somebody else's work and read a good book. Thanks to the power company that produced the air conditioning I enjoyed today and the radio station employees who worked on a holiday.

September 4: Retired or Laid Off,

"Nobody can ride your back if your back's not bent," Dr. Martin Luther King Jr. said. Unfortunately, I know several people nearing retirement age that have been laid off or pushed into retiring early because of the economy. Although they have given many years to their employers, taking care of them doesn't seem to be part of the modern corporate or nonprofit culture. Not surprisingly they feel badly even if they know in their hearts it isn't about them.

September 5: It's So Daily!
Freedom is like taking a bath - you have to keep doing it every day!
—Flo Kennedy

Today I went to have my yearly mammogram. All check-in and technician staff needed several reminders: talk to me, and not the sighted person I am with, and do not pet the dog. Instead of pointing and saying "there," tap the chair to show me where it is. Please don't send me a letter with results—call. By the last person, I was making a game of it with myself; how can I get the healthcare provider to be interested in figuring out accessibility instead of me bossing her with "do this, don't do that." Before, my heart just wasn't into doing public education. But I wanted access, so I did it. Just like freedom or taking a bath, access is so daily!

For the second act I fiddled with a fundraising website where I tried to contribute to a friend's ride to benefit Seeing Eye. The "submit" button didn't have an alt text tag on it, so I could fill out the donation form, but not submit it. I found an 800 number, gave my information over the phone and suggested the gal tell the website designer what needed changing. She said she would. I'll check it next year, if Tom rides again. A five-minute task took ninety minutes.

September 6: Courage
Courage is doing what you're afraid to do. There can be no courage unless you're scared.—Eddie Rickenbacker

This week I listened to a TED Talk by Candy Chang. She lives in New Orleans and loves it passionately. In 2009, her dear friend died suddenly and it made her think a lot. There are many abandoned buildings there, and on one in her neighborhood she stenciled "Before I die I want to…" on one wall. By the end of the day it was full of answers; some big and some small. Since then she's continued this neighborhood project. What would yours be? The first one to come to mind for me is being a member of the fifty-year club at Seeing Eye. Right now that involves the courage to try new routes and new situations with Luna.

September 7: Virtues of Procrastinating

John Perry, Emeritus Professor of Philosophy at Stanford University has written *The Art of Procrastination: A Guide to Effective Lollygagging, and Postponing*. Hearing it discussed on Wisconsin Public Radio today made me think. Over the years I've counseled many people about how to cut down on their procrastination tendencies. Since I'm the kind of person who gets the dentist over with at 8:00 AM if that's possible, I have little empathy for procrastinators. It was good for me to consider advantages of procrastinating, like having more time to gather information for decision-making and letting others jump in and do a task so I don't have to. Maybe I'll think more about this subject—but not now.

September 8: Inspiration Comes From Many Places

I was glancing through *Power of Two: Surviving a Serious Illness with Attitude and an Advocate* by G. Monaghan. It was written by the wife of a cancer survivor. It has great tips, websites, and a booklist that guide you through a serious illness of your own or that of a loved one. What struck me most was the inclusion of a list of books her husband found inspiring (including *Seabiscuit* written by a gal with chronic fatigue) and a few of her husband's favorite Irish jokes. These are people it would be fun to know!

While out delivering pet food and boxes of kitty litter, one of my favorite songs, "All God's Creatures Have a Place in the Choir" came on the radio.
All God's creatures have a place in the choir,
Some sing low, some sing higher,
Some sing out loud on the telephone wire,
Some just clap their hands, or paws, or anything
Inspiration does come from many places.

September 9: Care and Feeding of Friends

Enjoying friendships is one of the best things about aging. Not that I didn't enjoy them before, but now I have more time and energy to engage in the proper care and feeding of friendships. Some of the care and feeding I did today included: sharing a book review, cooking a special dish, sending a thank you e-mail, taking a walk and listening, phoning a friend and listening, and praying for friends' needs. E-mails, garden produce, a funny article about the head Marine Corps dog behaving badly but still getting promoted, and several fine conversations came back. There's also the friendship with my new Seeing Eye dog. In addition to the necessities of food, water and potty breaks, we walked, played keep away with her bone, and she got a belly rub. I got good guide service and some wonderful licks. It's harder to reach out and make new friends as I age, maybe because of laziness. Again I'm reminded of the song I learned in Brownies, "Make new friends, but keep the old. One is silver and the other's gold."

September 10: Rin Tin Tin's Birthday

From humble beginnings, being a soldier's friend, Rin Tin Tin became a movie star. How did this happen? Luck? A cute face? Smart? Being in the right place at the right time? Hardworking? Just like the rest of us, a combination of all of the above. Look at the interesting life he had! Since Luna's birthday is on Groundhog Day and I didn't know her then, I decided she could have a biscuit on Rin Tin Tin's birthday. Live it up is her motto!

September 11: National Day of Service and Remembrance

I've had wonderful opportunities for service, ranging from writing for a Braille women's magazine, to serving on city, county, and state boards; mentoring blind students; giving talks to groups from three-year-olds to nursing home residents; reading scripture and starting a book club at church; and founding a pet food program for disabled and elderly people. I've started awards for children's books about the disability experience and good disability issues journalism. Then there's the baking for good causes and helping with fundraisers. They aren't something I invented, but I sure can and do participate. I get great joy out of meeting a real human need, or even a cat's need for boxes of kitty litter!

Too often people with disabilities stop themselves from volunteering for several reasons: nobody asks them, they don't know where to start, and they don't think they have anything to give. I think we're in a unique spot to give help because we know about particular needs and have figured out tricks of the trade to deal with them. We should be on the boards of disability and aging-related organizations. National Day of Service is a great day to remind ourselves of Kennedy's quote, "Ask not what your country can do for you, but what you can do for your country." That's true for all of us.

September 12: Being Twice as Good

When I read this about race, I thought, "Well said for disability."

Atlantic Senior Editor Ta-Nehisi Coates writes in his recent piece "Fear of a Black President.," that in order to achieve full integration, blacks must be "twice as good but half as black." Growing up, I knew I had to be better than a sighted person to get a job. My parents told me "Don't act blind." In their eyes, overcome your disability, or be a loser on welfare seemed to be the only two choices. Simon and Garfunkel's song "I Am a Rock" was my theme song. In middle age, after proving myself to anybody I could find to prove myself to, I began to realize I wanted more. I wanted friends, hobbies, fun, and relaxation (whatever that was). I met some people with disabilities who weren't quite as far out on the prove yourself 24/7 continuum as I was and began to inch toward a more relaxed stance.

September 13: Vulnerability

Brene Brown, author of *Daring Greatly: How the Courage to Be Vulnerable Transforms the Way We Live, Love, Parent, and Lead* presents an alternative to yesterdays be twice as good motif. A few examples of both strength and vulnerability include: Christopher Hitchins, who at the end of a successful career wrote his last book *Mortality* about his cancer; rising classical pianist Nicholas McCarthy, who was born with only a left hand; Oscar Pistorius the "Blade-Runner" who competed both in Olympics and Paralympics; and Cathy Birchall, the first blind woman to ride round the world on the back of a motorcycle. Her fiancé Bernard Smith was the driver. Their book about their travels is called *Touching the World*. The more I admit my vulnerability and ask for needed help clearly and unapologetically, the better the results are. The first million times are the hardest!

September 14: Happier

In *Happier at Home: Kiss More, Jump More, Abandon a Project, Read Samuel Johnson,* and *My Other Experiments in the Practice of Everyday Life* Gretchen Rubin advocate doing some little things to make life happier at home that don't cost much or take much time. In that spirit, I'm ordering out Chinese tonight with no better excuse than the outside of the house is getting painted. I'm not sure how that relates! Then I'll settle in for Friday night with a thriller, *The American* by Britton.

This evening a neighbor was walking into their house carrying pumpkin cheesecake and Luna almost fell over backwards trying to see if she would get some. She was sure it would make her happier. I guess she'll have to make do with a game of bone tug-of-war with me instead.

September 15: Spiritual Aging

Keeping Spiritual Balance As We Grow Older: More than 65 Creative Ways to Use Purpose, Prayer, and the Power of Spirit to Build a Meaningful Retirement" by Molly and Bernie Srode is a great introduction to what I need to be doing spiritually. I find myself squirming as I think about any of Jung's seven tasks of aging spiritually, but I guess squirming is better than just not thinking about them. They are: facing the reality of aging and dying, life review, coming to peace with life, moving the focus from ego to others, spiritual self becomes more important, finding the meaning of one's life and death so you're comfortable with living and dying. Life is certainly giving me losses and opportunities to make meaning and a little more patience with reflection. Keeping a daily journal is very helpful in that area.

September 16: Upcycling

Danny Seo has written a book called *Upcycling Celebrations.* He is one of America's leading lifestyle authorities on modern, eco-friendly living. But my mom taught me to do upcycling before there was a word for it. We unwrapped presents carefully so the paper could be reused. We also cut off the fronts of greeting cards so they could decorate a trash can or be put in scrapbooks for nursing home residents to look at.

I wish I could think of something to do to upcycle old magazines on cassettes. At least with old braille magazines they can be put out for curbside recycling. I've got enough stacks of deli containers waiting to be upcycled to fill at least one cupboard. I need to balance upcycling with just plain throwing things away.

Do I get points for upcycling when I regift? Maybe I could use those points to justify just plain tossing some stuff.

September 17: Philanthropy Talk

Today I went to hear Jim Pinter, a local man give a talk titled, "My Seventy-Five Year Personal Journey of Life and Philanthropy." He clearly met the definition of a philanthropist, giving his time, talents and money to the United Way, Rotary, Eau Claire Community Foundation and more. He talked about the sources of his thinking, including many business and personal motivation luminaries. He described prayer, purpose, planning, and positive imaging among other pillars of his thinking. He was humble enough to admit he didn't always live up to his own lofty aspirations. This man is well on the way to achieving what Erma Bombeck once said, "When I stand before God at the end of my life, I'd hope that I would not have a single bit of talent left and could say, 'I used everything you gave me.'"

One new tidbit for me was the Platinum Rule: treat others the way they want to be treated. In some situations I could see that working well. For example, when I entered a gathering of the Women's Giving Circle today, I wanted food described instead of just being welcomed and waved toward the table. I ended up asking, "Is there food?" and when told yes, asking "What's there?" At that point the gal in charge of hospitality asked, "Should I get you some?" "Yes" I replied, "that would be great."

In this organization I want to "be the change" as Lisa Endlich has described it. But first I will have to fit in. Several gals thanked me for coming and were visibly surprised when I said that I was a new member. I'll have to show up, rub elbows, and talk common bond topics like dogs and recipes. Then maybe I can move them toward justice with instead of charity for "the less fortunate". Occupying philanthropy will be a piece of ongoing work. "The Impossible Will Take a Little While" as Billie Holliday said.

September 18: Dog Stories

I heard today that Norman Bridwell's beloved *Clifford the Big Red Dog* turns fifty this year. His stories walk children through baths, first day of school, holidays, cooperating and many other life events and tasks.

Two Plus Four Equals One: Celebrating the Partnership of People with Disabilities and Their Assistance Dogs by Kathy Nimmer contains short, funny, and touching accounts of the effect guide dogs and service dogs have had on their owners' lives. Both Clifford and the dogs described in Nimmer's book truly make life better for their people. I'm so excited that Kathy will be coming to Eau Claire next month to participate in our book festival and do a couple of school talks. She seems like someone who appreciates the magic of the relationship between a dog and a human and can share that.

September 19: Visiting the Dying
When you come to the edge of all that you know,
you must believe in one of two things:
Either there will be earth on which to stand,
or you will be given wings.
—O.R. Melling

Today I visited a dying child and her family. I didn't want to go. I felt totally inadequate to say or do anything helpful. But I baked bars and, knew that there would be good in it, somehow. It turns out it was meant to be. When I arrived, the teenage sibling of the dying child was bolting out of the room as fast as possible, with hurt and anger about her sister's impending death clearly rolling off her. Luna lunged to greet her and just kept wagging and pawing at her until she leaned down and accepted the love. No human could have shown her love at that moment, but she took it from Luna.

September 20: Circles of Care
You can do something I can't do. I can do something you can't do. Together let us do something beautiful for God.
—Mother Teresa

"Nothing Gold Can Stay"
By Robert Frost

Nature's first green is gold,
Her hardest hue to hold.
Her early leaf's a flower;
But only so an hour.
Then leaf subsides to leaf.
So Eden sank to grief,
So dawn goes down to day.
Nothing gold can stay.

The young blind child I've mentored died today. As I think about her family, her teachers, her music therapist, and the community that pitched in for fundraisers, I'm struck by how many did their best for her. Her life was way too short. But, it was "good" as she'd always say when someone asked how she was. I'm sure she's up in heaven beating St. Peter at Ned's Head, a game she was passionate about down here. I don't know whether she's using her cane to get around heaven, or whether she has normal vision, but I'm sure she is pain-free and whole. Helen Keller said, "What we have once enjoyed we can never lose. All that we love deeply becomes a part of us." My young friend's love of life was infectious. I'll miss collecting riddles to spring on her.

September 21: The Joys of Fall

I'll leave it to others to rhapsodize about the visual, but here are some of my favorite sensory experiences of fall:

Taste: tart but sweet apple cider (hot or cold), curried butternut squash soup, the last batch of homegrown little tomatoes, candy corn mixed with peanuts (highly addictive) and stuffing (even vegetarian);

Touch: crunching through leaves on the ground, touching the flannel sheets going back on the bed, feeling the warm sun on my face followed by a cool breeze;

Smell: pumpkin innards when you're just starting to carve the pumpkin, burning leaves, and apple pie baking;

Sounds: listening to the swish of walking through leaves, geese honking to each other, marching bands practicing for football games, and kids yelling, "trick or treat!"

September 22: Is Going to Mass a Duty or Entertainment?

A lonely young blind man I e-mail with asked me what I was going to do for entertainment today. I listed several things, including going to Mass. He said he thought that was a duty, not an entertainment. Here's what I wrote him later that day:

Sure enough, Mass qualified as entertainment! First there was the beauty of walking over there on a cool but sunny fall day, scuffing through leaves. Then there was watching Luna decide to do the right thing and turn up the walk to church instead of going past and getting in trouble, which she fleetingly considered. Then the whole back row gang was there. In the gang are a single man who is a housepainter, a retired nursery school teacher, a sweet couple married for forty-nine years (both of whom have serious health issues), and Luna and me. Before Mass, we discussed: where to get quilt calendars, what color to paint a bed for a grandkid, when the ladies of the back row could go out to lunch, and a game on one of the gal's iPhones called Fruit Ninja. She barely got it turned off before we rose for the first song. During the passing of the peace, the husband gave his wife a big, noisy kiss. The homily was about getting what you need from God, not always what you want. The priest usually ends with a question of the week. This time the question was what are you going to ask God for this week to make you a better person and a better disciple? When we got home, Luna had been so good for so long that she ran around the house in circles for five minutes. All in all, quite entertaining! There was some beauty, some laughs, some community, and something to think about.

September 23: Getting Ready for Banned Books Week

For over thirty years, the last week in September has been designated as Banned Books Week. According to the American Library Association:

Banned Books Week is an annual event celebrating the freedom to read and the importance of the First Amendment. Banned Books Week highlights the benefits of free and open access to information while drawing attention to the harms of censorship by spotlighting actual or attempted banning's of books across the United States. The books featured during Banned Books Week have been targets of attempted banning's. Fortunately, while some books were banned or restricted, in a majority of cases the books were not banned.

I've celebrated in previous years by volunteering to read from a banned book at a celebration. I've realized that in addition to banning, another form of censorship is not providing the book in an accessible format. For example, when I was growing up, Nancy Drew books were not available in Braille or on tape. I didn't know what the other girls were talking about when they discussed them. I know government funds were limited so mainly "great" literature was made accessible. I'm grateful I could read books like *Little Women*. Nowadays, with the advent of Bookshare and Learning Ally, much more reading material is available to people with print disabilities. For example, within a week of its publication in regular print, J. K. Rowling's first novel for adults, *Casual Vacancy* was posted on Bookshare. There are certainly many books I'd like to read that are still not available. For instance, *Winter Journal* was only available for a while for Canadian users of Bookshare because of copyright issues. Now it has become available for U.S. users. When I wanted to attend a series on Yeats at my public library, I had to get the handouts and then search for the poems individually on the Internet to find accessible versions.

Few publishers publish books in large print. Friends of mine who read large print have few choices. Many can't or don't want to invest in or learn to use an iDevice where you can enlarge print. Having already read *50 Shades of Gray*, which never would have been available in the bad old days, I think I'll look at the list of most frequently challenged books and pick one. *Hunger Games* is on this year's list, and we'll be discussing it in a book club I'm in. Since it is available in alternate format, let the reading begin!

September 24: Uberty

Today is the birthday of Blind Lemon Jefferson. He was born Lemon Henry Jefferson to sharecroppers in Couchman, Texas in 1893. This blues great died thirty-six years later after recording over one hundred songs. He may have died in a snowstorm after losing his way. He was buried in an unmarked grave. A marker was erected thirty years later. He never achieved much fame or fortune. I learned the meaning of "uberty" today—fruitfulness. Obviously, Blind Lemon Jefferson was fruitful even though he didn't have a lot of worldly advantages. He is a good example of making something out of what you've got.

September 25: Shel Silverstein's Birthday

What a man! He wrote travel pieces for *Playboy* and wonderful books for kids like *The Giving Tree*. His book of poetry for children, *Where the Sidewalk Ends*, is a book I'd love to buy in Braille, but it isn't for sale as far as I know. Just consider these fragments from his poem "No Difference":

Rich as a sultan,
Poor as a mite,
We're all worth the same
When we turn off the light....

So maybe the way
To make everything right
Is for God to just reach out
And turn off the light!

September 26: Vegetarian Forever, I Hope

I've been a vegetarian for almost forty years now. I started when I was getting ready to get my first guide dog and realized some people eat dogs. That made me think about eating other animals, and the more I thought about it, the less appealing it became.   According to a 2008 *Vegetarian Times* study, 7.3 million Americans are vegetarians, and an additional 22.8 million follow a vegetarian-inclined diet. Things have gotten better for us over the years. More prepared vegetarian foods are available in grocery stores for us lazy vegetarians. Restaurants and conference meals now offer more vegetarian options. A few vegetarian cookbooks are even available in alternate format nowadays. About seventeen percent of us are fifty-five and older. I hope this means that when we get to living in assisted living and nursing home facilities, staff will be more aware of vegetarian diets than they currently are. At the facilities I visit, people are willing to do a grilled cheese or a peanut butter and jelly sandwich. That could get old quickly if you live there. Hopefully, as we Boomers occupy aging, we'll bring our vegetarianism with us.

September 27: Stuff

A couple un-clutters their life, gets off the corporate racetrack, and moves into a 128-square-foot house; wow! This is chronicled in

You Can Buy Happiness (and It's Cheap): How One Woman Radically Simplified Her Life and How You Can Too by Tammy Strobel.

I think about un-cluttering every time I visit friends in assisted living or nursing homes, but I keep putting it off. I have piles of magazines I was sure I'd get to when I retired. I have teaching notes that are twenty years old. I need to find a few small things I can do and just start with them. Moving helps, but I don't want to move any time soon. My main excess is information in accessible format; you can tell what I was starved for when I was young! Now I hoard it.

September 28: Fun with a Trip Report

I have fun letting my Seeing Eye dog craft letters and trip reports sometimes. Here's today's trip report (dictated by Luna):

The first unusual thing that happened was Kathie gave me vanilla-flavored Kaopectate on top of a few extra kibbles one night after I'd had diarrhea for three days. She assured me it was much tastier than when she was young. She used to run and hide and lie to not have to take it. The next day she packed essentials like my food and her laptop into her knapsack and off we went for an adventure. We went to Wausau for a Wisconsin Public Radio Association meeting. It was six hours of meetings each of two days, where I slept and woke up, and people were still talking. At one point I did wake up to hear bear cubs squealing on a recording of some story they played from WPR to illustrate how hours of tape were honed down into a ninety-second story. If you ask me, they could hone those meetings down in a similar fashion. It was my first meeting like that, so I just slept and behaved perfectly. The hotel put us near a back door where a nice private plot of grass was available for my use within fifty feet of the door. That magic, vanilla-flavored medicine did its part, and I got through the night with only one trip outside. The next day there were more meetings but no tape of bear cubs, and I was home in time for dinner. After dining (always my first priority) I ran around the house for five minutes and then went outside to take care of nature's call in my own yard. Truly, there is no place like home. After two months with Kathie, I do know where my home is. I know you are my friend and would want to know that I survived the world of long meetings masquerading as retreats'.

—Luna

September 29: Giving from the Heart

Today I did one of my favorite Saturday activities: I went to the farmers' market. The day was a perfect, early fall, crisp and clear day. The café that sells egg rolls was still there; next week is their last week of the season. I went to pick out six gourds for little gifts for this week. One is for the gal who delivers home delivery library books for me, two for a birthday lunch, and three for gals who will help me with the pet food delivery next weekend. But, after having great fun pawing through all the gourds to pick a selection, things took an interesting turn. I went to pay and the Hmong farmer said "no." He was giving them to me. I said no, I'll pay, and he said no, and tapped his heart and said "gift from the heart." Clearly he knew the truth of this quote:

No one has ever become poor by giving.
—Anne Frank

I thanked him many times and was moving off when he added a bag of potatoes to his gift. I will share the potatoes with guests on Monday and have a wonderful story to tell each recipient of a gourd. A bit of me squirms at the thought of him giving them to me because I'm blind, but the gesture felt generous, not slimy and condescending. I'll just be thankful.

When we give cheerfully and accept gratefully, everyone is blessed.
—Maya Angelou

September 30: From "Grrr" to a Gift?

A wheelchair-using friend almost didn't get Communion brought to her today! We discussed the next church social event (held in the inaccessible basement of the church) and how we could make it happen accessibly. If it's held upstairs or waiter service is offered, people who don't do stairs could still easily participate and get food brought up for them without having it be a major issue. Grrr! My blood pressure rises as I think of a church community not being fully accessible and inattentive to these issues.

Sometimes a book pops up right when it needs to, and it sure did today. I was reading the book *Unexpected Gifts* by Richard Rohr and Christopher L Heuertz and this quote really struck me;

144

"Ironically, as much as we yearn for deep friendships and meaningful communities, many of us seem to be unable to find our way into them. Even if we know we're made for community, finding one and staying there seems almost impossible. Though we hate to admit it, if we stay long enough in any relationship or set of friendships, we will experience failure, doubt, burnout, loneliness, transitions, and a loss of self, betrayal, frustration, a sense of entitlement, grief, and weariness."

The book grabbed me right from the introduction! Amen on the frustration! Now how to see it as a gift? I must read on. The authors seem to suggest I should find a common bond with the person I have the conflict with and build on it. They also suggest a bridge person who is well-connected with the community and with whom I'm connected. A couple people spring to mind on the inaccessible parties in the basement issue. I have to trust them, and I have to accept that they may not get it done *my way* or even score a home run the first time. I need to celebrate their efforts anyway. The "grrr" is morphing into a revving of my engines!

☽

October 1: Blindness Awareness Month

October is Blindness Awareness Month. Forty-four states recognize October 2012 as Blindness Awareness Month. Initiated by the Little Rock Foundation, it is a campaign aimed at educating and enlightening others about blindness. It all began with a blind New Jersey teenager named Rocco Fiorentino. I have lecture opportunities to spread awareness to over five hundred people this month about issues faced by people who are blind. I wonder what other opportunities will present themselves. Maybe I should figure out something cute to post on Facebook and blog about it.

October 2: Somebody with Blindness Awareness Educates Me

As I walked across campus today to go to the bank, one of the groundskeepers stopped me to warn me about a hole in the path where they were going to plant a tree. When queried about what they were planting, he said "Kentucky coffee bean tree." I admitted to never having heard of it. He told me the tree was kind of like the honey locust, and the beans were used by Native Americans as game pieces. He didn't know why it was called "coffee bean". When I googled it, it turns out that early settlers used it as a substitute for coffee, but it is poisonous in large amounts so they gave it up as soon as they could get the real thing. An encounter that started out as an example of someone with good instincts about being helpful to blind travelers ended up educating me about a kind of tree I'd never heard of. Helped and educated; not bad for a two-minute encounter! Since it's one of my heroes' birthday today, Mahatma Gandhi, I'll end with a Gandhi quote: "Live as if you were to die tomorrow. Learn as if you were to live forever."

October 3: Time Enough?

I finished reading Mitch Albom's *Time Keeper* today. It's an interesting short novel about wishing for more time. The book made me question myself about what I put off and why. Do I live the moment? Or, do I say "give me more time"? When someone asked me to gather old pictures for a display and get quotes for T-shirts for a project, I easily said "no". If I'd been asked by a boss to do those tasks, I would have, but as a volunteer I felt free to say "not me". Not everybody would ask a blind person to find old photos and pick and choose which ones to display. Instead of getting indignant, I've had fun telling the story and laughing with friends—a much better use of my time.

October 4: St. Francis and Me

St. Francis danced and sang in the streets. He embraced simplicity and nonviolence. He treasured creatures and vulnerable beings. I celebrated his day by playing with Luna, going out to lunch with two friends, and taking supper to a family whose child died a few weeks ago. Supper wasn't grand, just tuna casserole and chocolate chip cookies—the kind of food Francis would have liked. On Sunday we'll get Luna blessed along with two of my retired guide dogs. I need to bake zucchini bread for the owners and cook for two potlucks this weekend. I wonder who cooked for the first Franciscans?

October 5: Learning in Retirement

When I retired, I pictured myself taking occasional classes as an auditor (no tests, thank you!) at the university like a friend of mine does. I haven't done it yet. I don't wish to be tied down that much. We are blessed with so many opportunities in Eau Claire: free classes at the library, senior center, churches, and (for a small charge) Chippewa Valley Learning in Retirement. My favorites have been poetry offerings at the library. Skill classes like Ceramics and Improv haven't worked because of disability issues. There's also independent learning from reading a book, or surfing the net. Hadley School for the Blind offers free seminars by phone on blindness-related skills and topics. I may offer to do one on volunteering. I'm reading about MOOCs (massive open online courses). When I checked for a poetry MOOC, the website wanted me to upgrade my browser, and I wondered how that would go with my screen reader. I'll probably read a book instead. I do love the contact with other learners in the library classes; it's inspiring to see so many of us working to keep our minds exercised.

October 6: Miracles

There are two ways to live your life. One is as though nothing is a miracle. The other is as though everything is a miracle.
—Albert Einstein

The word "miracle" means something that happens because of supernatural intervention, or a wonderful event according to Dictionary.com. I did a bit of research on the latter definition. Whether you come at it from a Christian or a New Age perspective, you can, as Regina Brett's book is titled, *Be the Miracle*. Increasing awareness, being grateful, and common self-help strategies like "do your best and forget the rest" are suggested.

October 7: Being Blessed and a Wisconsin Picnic

In Numbers 6 the Israelites learn to bless as follows: "The LORD bless you and keep you; the LORD make His face shine upon you, and be gracious to you; the LORD lift up His countenance upon you, and give you peace." Rarely am I blessed or do I bless others any way but by saying "bless you" when someone sneezes. It's a great thing to wish power, encouragement, peace, and joy to people, but it's just not something I'm comfortable doing. Somehow, though, when a holy man like Father Klimek blesses the animals, and the people who care for them, it feels good. At today's Blessing of the Animals, even the animals seemed to know and not pick too serious quarrels with each other as they waited in line for the blessing. As usual, there were about forty-five dogs and a couple of cats there. Whether it was the cool and breezy weather, or the Packer game in progress, attendance was down a little.

Later in the day, I went to a neighborhood picnic. I took a summery salad, as did many others. The weather had turned to fall, but we sat outside anyway. When I got home, I checked and it was thirty-seven degrees. Only in Wisconsin would you sit outside with light jackets on for a picnic at that temperature. The neighborhood kids were inside, though I'm not sure if that was because of the warmth or the access to Wii and other electronic entertainment. In any case, I was blessed with good food and neighborhood camaraderie. Near the end, Luna whimpered. I figured she was cold, but it turned out the cold had made her bladder active, and she needed to go. She got blessed relief as soon as we crossed the street.

October 8: Play

After doing some work, Luna and I came home and played a game of chase around the living/dining room. It was good stress release for both of us and gave me some stretching, balancing, and work on my reflexes. Luna was faster than me but my strategy for blocking her was better. The pure abandon with which she played made me laugh. It reminds me of my Friday night bridge games—there's thinking about the cards, but there's also plenty of trash talk and friendly mocking of the opposition. I'm glad I have a young dog and old friends who like to play; both keep me lively.

October 9: Books and Hope

I did a book review for the morning reading group I'm in (average age eighty-plus). I decided to do books about hope. I did an informal survey of LISTSERVs and friends for nominations. Memoirs of people who overcome great obstacles like *Life is so Good* (about the grandson of a slave who learned to read at ninety-eight) and *Left Neglected* (about living with a stroke) were suggested. So were psychological self-help books like books by Leo Buscaglia and *Active Hope: How to Face the Mess* by Joanna Macy. Historical fiction like *Little House on the Prairie* and *Oh Pioneer* were nominated. One gal mentioned *Gift from the Sea* by Lindbergh and *The Prophet* by Gibran. Mitch Albom's and Richard Paul Evans' latest and Christian fiction authors like Karen Kingsbury were mentioned. One person suggested *Tin Roof Blowdown* by James Lee Burke. It's a gritty police novel with more bad guys than good guys. However, the man who suggested the book felt it had hope in it because sometimes even the bad guys did good things.

I talked about *Pilgrimage into the Last Third of Life* and gave an example of the discussion questions at the end of each chapter. The chapter on living with limitations included the question: "How can you glorify God in your limitations?" I'm still meditating on that one. The book club ladies left with smiles on their faces. That may well have been the result of fellowship and the home-baked pecan rolls.

October 10: Inspired by a Young Girl's Activism

The news today had a story about Malala Yousafzai, a fifteen year-old Pakistani girl who was shot in the head by the Taliban because of her activism for girls' education. She was quoted in the *Christian Science Monitor* as saying, "don't worry, Baba. I am going to be fine and victory will be ours." What an amazing example of courage for something I can easily take lightly, an education. In addition to praying for her recovery, I honored her by calling the Braille student I mentor, and started soliciting ideas for an educational pamphlet.

My student is a middle-aged man who didn't graduate from high school while sighted, but now wants to learn to read Braille and get his GED. I call him every two weeks and act as his "education nag". Today I celebrated with him his first certificate for a series of lessons completed. The certificate was in both Braille and print. A few more lessons and he'll earn a Braille labeler so he can label cans and other household items.

O Magazine's article "101 best pieces of advice" from the October 2012 issue contained these nuggets that jumped out at me:

"You can only go as fast as the slowest part of you can go."
—from an unnamed therapist

Don't ever confuse—your life and your work. The second is only part of the first.
—Anna Quindlen

Since it is Blindness Awareness month, I put a call out on my LIST-SERVs for their best advice for sighted people about interacting with blind and visually impaired people. Stay tuned for the results.

October 11: Falling Apart

It's not a good omen when the day after the plumber is here to fix the toilet, the chain won't stay hooked, and so the flush mechanism won't work. After wiring it together myself, (we'll see how long it takes it to rust through) I went to the dentist. The last few months thorough brushing has not been my highest priority and it showed. I racked up a few cavities. I'll have to go back for an extra visit. This involves finding a sitter for Luna. , She charmed the socks off the gal who stayed with her today, so I think that may be taken care of. Even though I keep working with the dentist's staff, they talk about me as much as they talk to me, and pat me reassuringly as they redo X-rays. It's a dismal experience all in all. To contrast with my funk about falling apart, I read *Drop Dead Healthy*. The author who has already lived a year following every rule in the Bible, decides to "get healthy". He subjected himself to a grueling regimen of exercises, a range of diets, and an array of practices to improve everything from his hearing, to his sleep, to his sex life. Just reading about some of the crazy things he tried left me laughing and thinking that falling apart might be preferable.

October 12: Important People

Listening to a talk by John St. Augustine about his book, *Living an Uncommon Life: Essential Lessons from 21 Extraordinary People* started me thinking about who those people were in my life. My parents, several teachers and professors immediately came to my mind. They taught their subjects but also cared about their students. Many friends have enriched my life. One time my brother who is sighted asked "How come you have so many friends?" Maybe part of it is being female, but I'm also sure part of it is being blind. I need to interact with people to get help, and sometimes those interactions turn into friendships. That's one of the good things about my disability. I call these good things "pearls" and try to talk about them when I'm doing disability awareness talks. Too often people think of the negatives, which are there surely. There is also a need to remember the positive things as well.

October 13: Tattoos

I don't have a tattoo but was amazed to hear that forty percent of Americans between the ages of thirty and forty do. This also made me think of the jokes about what tattoos gotten when young will look like after the stretching, sagging, and wrinkling of aging. If I did get a tattoo, what would it be? A heart with a guide dog in harness on it, a cross, a crow, a book with a finger reading Braille, a musical note, friends around a table enjoying a good meal I'd cooked, the ace of spades…

October 14: Finishing Strong

Lately I've been around several people who have died or are dying. A friend just told me cancer is back again and this round it may win. She like others I know will finish strong. In *Coming Back Stronger*, Drew Brees, a football player who survived a tough childhood, a career-threatening shoulder injury, and his town being underwater from Hurricane Katrina, talks about what it takes to finish strong. Some of the things he mentions are; faith, friends and family, and an attitude built over a lifetime of just doing it one day at a time. He points out that sometimes you do go backward, but that can be a way to get ready to jump over a chasm. My friend is looking forward to time with family, enjoying reading, and learning all she can about her treatment. I wonder what she's doing with her terror. Other than dropping open-ended questions into the chitchat, and hoping she'll pick up on them if she wants, I don't know what to do. I hope to show up with food soon. Her husband talks about the weather with me when I call, and then turns me over to her. I have no idea where men go with their feelings, especially men of our generation that weren't encouraged to talk about them.

October 15: Happy White Cane Safety Day Celebrated with a Yellow Guide Dog

My Haiku says:
a cane or a dog
Shows you you need to take care
And makes me safer.

The law says: "An operator of a vehicle shall stop the vehicle before approaching closer than 10feet to a pedestrian who is carrying a cane or walking stick which is white in color or white trimmed with red and which is held in an extended or raised position or who is using a dog guide and shall take such precautions as may be necessary to avoid accident or injury to the pedestrian."

In 1964 Congress designated October 15 as White Cane Safety Day. On October 14, 2011, the president designated October 15th as "Blind Americans Equality Day." He said: "Generations of blind and visually impaired Americans have dedicated their passion and skills to enhancing our national life-leading as public servants, penning works of literature, lending their voice to music, and inspiring as champions of sport. On Blind Americans Equality Day, we celebrate the achievements of blind and visually impaired Americans and reaffirm our commitment to advancing their complete social and economic integration." (Proclamation 8739)

Luna and I celebrated by taking a walk in the neighborhood on a beautiful fall day. I must have been wool-gathering, because we got turned around, and only had a general idea of where we were. But our teamwork triumphed and we got home to continue the celebrating with a short game of chase, followed by a nap in the sun for the four-footed member of the team. It's moments of teamwork, where I'm suggesting directions, and a known destination like "home" and my guide dog is using her intelligence to keep me safe while finding the destination, that take traveling from a chore to a fun adventure.

However you say it and however you celebrate it: Happy White Cane Day!

October 16: Busy Day
Nobody finds time for prayer. You either take time for it or you don't get it.
—Joan Chittister

Today I guest lectured at two classes, and served dinner to guests. Back when I was working that would have been a light day. Today it seemed like too much and I was almost rushing. I was still able to get in walks and games with Luna, but no novel reading until bedtime, and barely a "thanks God" for prayer time. I'm glad this is an exceptional day for me. Naps, friends, music, and prayer take time!

October 17: Beauty is a verb

What an intriguing title: *Beauty is a Verb: the New Poetry of Disability* is. Bartlett, Black and Northern have assembled a variety of poems, directly and indirectly about disabilities from the mid-20th century on. Some of my favorites are: "If I Had Wheels or Love," "Poet of Cripples," "Normal," and "Poems with Disabilities". The last is a mock of justifications for "handicapped parking" spots even if none of those people are around. Daniel Simpson's (a poet who is blind) "Line Breaks as I see Them" was a wonderful reminder to me to write from my own experience, and not try to make myself into a sighted writer. Wolf's "Helen Keller Poems" resonates with my love/hate relationship with this remarkable, complex woman who was held up as a plaster saint throughout my youth. Clark's "Translating and Reading ASL Poems" was truly educational to me. Bartlett's meditation on the ethics of disability and her preference to be a "good poet who has a disability," rather than a disability poet, mirrors my struggles about my disability and aging identities. Many of the poems are pleasing to the ear, hence beautiful. Chapman and Strasser have compiled a good anthology on retirement. I wonder who will do the many hours of work to put together an anthology like this on aging?

October 18: A Big and Wonderful Day

Sometimes the stars align and a day just couldn't be better. Six months of planning and working with various constituencies brought the fourth annual Disability Issues Forum to fruition. This year's speaker, Kathy Nimmer, an English teacher and author of *Two Plus Four Equals One* — about assistance dogs, wowed her audience of about one hundred and seventy-five people, three assistance dogs in training, and Luna. My brunch for the speaker turned out perfectly. The dinner for her, and other Chippewa Valley Book Festival authors was excellent and the other speaker I heard was interesting. From each talk I also gathered ideas of things to do differently in my talks, like summarize my main points at the end. I served, learned, and just plain enjoyed, all in one day. I even got most of my e-mail thank you's sent before falling into bed. Thank you God for the strength to insist that I bring this speaker; she touched many people deeply.

October 19: Would it Kill You to Stop Doing That?

Would It Kill You to Stop Doing That: is a modern guide to manners by Henry Alford. Manners have changed with the times, and I was intrigued with suggestions on how to discreetly find out who a found cell phone belongs to if there's no identifying information in it. You can call the last number dialed, but remember to be cautious because the person may be having an affair with the person at that number. There weren't many situations discussed involving elderly or people with disabilities. One situation that I'm going to have to find a gentle way to handle occurs in a monthly meeting. The chair always says "For Kathie's sake, let's all go around and say our names." The good news is they do, so I know who is where. But constantly having it pointed out that it's for my benefit grates on me. I may end up just e-mailing the chair and using the Schneider sandwich as some of my interns named it: compliment, request for change, compliment.

Then there's the "Can I call you Friday?" (no time named) question. It assumes that because I'm retired, I'm sitting there waiting for their call. I've learned to counter that with: "What time Friday would be good for you?"
My skills in graciously taking charge of awkward situations continually grow. The gracious part is where the growth needs to keep happening.

October 20: Taking Time

Because a friend's cancer has taken a turn for the worse, instead of saying let's do lunch sometime, three of us got together and "did lunch" today. The food was good and although we didn't solve any world problems, the chatter about books and life was fun. We all lived in the present for that brief time and enjoyed each other's presences. I sat in the car afterwards, warmed by the late fall sun while my friend who drove hunted down mint chocolate chips at the grocery store for a baking project. I was content to pet Luna and bask in the warm glow of friendship— be it canine or human.

October 21: Accepting Help

Haddayr Copley-Woods has been grappling with how to handle unwanted help since she was diagnosed with multiple sclerosis four years ago. In an interview on "To the Best of Our Knowledge" a Wisconsin Public Radio show, she talked about how emotionally exhausting it was to deal with the conflicting feelings of asking for, receiving and turning down help. Sometimes she feels angry when help is offered and she doesn't need it, but also she's angry when her husband doesn't do helpful things he knows she needs without her having to ask. She suggests people offer help when they think she is struggling. For having only been a disabled person the last four years, I think she's doing very well articulating some of the challenges of being a recipient of help. I want to tell her that after a while it does get less painful. Scabs develop on one's vulnerability that are not knocked off quite as easily. On a bad day, I can still leave a helping encounter licking my wounds and occasionally delivering a wound to the helper as well. Occasionally I have the grace to say "I'm sorry" or at least to pray for the grace to apologize the next time I snap.

October 22: Rallying the Troops

Nothing great in the world has been accomplished without passion.
 —G.W.F. Hegel

Because of various budget cuts there's talk that the hot meal provided to residents at an apartment building for low-income seniors and people with disabilities will be cut from five days a week to four. Knowing some of these people personally from years of delivering pet food and supplies to them, I'm angry about this. In the great scheme of things, it's only a few people and maybe some of them can go to the Community Table, maybe some will be able to receive Meals on Wheels, but they are losing a reason to get out of their apartments and wheel down to the lunch room. I called one of the most outspoken residents I know and talked with her about getting some people to testify at the county budget meeting. I was able to get a friend to say she'd take a carload of people to the meeting. I'll talk, but some residents would make it real to those who think "those people" really don't need this. The resident I know is optimistic she can gather several people if they're feeling okay that day. No snow on November 13 when we have to testify would be helpful too, for dragging walkers, canes, and oxygen bottles to the meeting. I worry if five days goes to four this year, what will happen next year? We'll howl anyway; it will not go unnoticed.

October 23: Almost as Good as Doing Graffiti

Because I'm blind I've never been able to read or write graffiti. Thirty years ago a few friends surveyed the campus and recorded some of the best graffiti for my listening pleasure. Wonderful! I understand most of it is stupid, vulgar and redundant, but enquiring minds do want to know.

Today I had the opportunity to sign the final cast concrete panel that will be placed atop a new campus building being built a half a block from my home. I signed it with my "Kathie and Luna" stamp and tried to paste Braille saying the same thing under it, but it wouldn't stick to the concrete. Others were enjoying signing the concrete and penning messages. One staff signed in honor of a faculty member who had died a year ago, and a student signed something about being one of those who helped pay for the building. This afternoon a crane will pick the beam up and place it on the roof. Luna's name will be there. Most of my dogs have had their names and paw prints on concrete when I had to get porch steps repaired, but Luna will be the first to have her name atop a building.

October 24: Occupying

Today I was reading *The Occupy Handbook* about the Occupy Wall Street movement. It is an anti-consumerist, anti-hierarchal, cultural-more–than-political movement. At its best people exchanged opinions and ideas about how to make America work better for the marginalized, not just the rich and famous. Although a few revered elders were there, it seemed to feature the young. Tactics like boycotts, giving the media political theater to cover and doing visible occupying remind me of the 1960's. I wonder how we can translate this to occupying institutions we as aging people care about. To me it starts with how we think about our lives, our disabilities, and our worth. Do we say "I'm old and I'm proud" in our words and actions? And what are our actions to occupy our work or volunteering, our friendships, our faith, and our play? On a larger level, how do we occupy our living facility, our city and county government, our nonprofits, and our national government, so the issues faced by elders are not marginalized? There is a lot of work to do, but there are forty million older Americans to help get the job done.

October 25: Tom Sullivan's Pearls

In his new book, *As I See It*, memoirist, singer and amazing man who is blind talks about the benefits of being blind. Some he names are:

I've never assessed my relationship with people according to the limits of labels or assumption.

I've enjoyed a world of senses available to all of us but almost never explored by the majority of those with sight.

I've made challenge my road to limitless opportunity.

I've cultivated a clear sense of my own purpose.

I've learned to be passionate, celebrating my own uniqueness through the expression of that passion.

I've found a powerful faith that has become my foundation for living.

I've learned to love unconditionally through the interdependent relationship I share with my wife, Patty, and my children.

Many of the pearls I'd name from my blindness are very similar. My interdependence is with a guide dog and friends, instead of a wife and kids, but it's the same song different verse. I'd also add the humorous things that happen because of my blindness or somebody else's sightedness.

October 26: A Real Christian

Today George McGovern was laid to rest and C-SPAN carried his funeral, including the bishop of the Dakotas and Minnesota's sermon. It was a beautiful tribute which talked about McGovern's peacemaking and work on world hunger. The bishop talked about Jesus' commands to feed the hungry and work toward peace and justice. He had a few funny stories from biographies of McGovern, and left listeners with the charge to do with their lives as McGovern had done with his. It was so wonderful compared to some funeral sermons I've heard lately; that are designed to scare the people who are there into getting right with God before they die. In my opinion, that's not the way to comfort the living.

October 27: Blind Bartimaeus

The Gospel reading was about Blind Bartimaeus asking Jesus for sight. The homily I heard said we all want to see God's handiwork (beauty in nature), God in each other, and God in the Eucharist. I've heard worse sermons about Blind Bartimaeus, but somehow I wish I would hear better. I'd like to hear someone highlight the fact that Bartimaeus knew enough to call out to Jesus even though he was a "blind beggar." I'd like to hear someone pointing out that he followed Jesus after his healing; a brave thing to do since Jesus was heading to his death soon after this incident. Apparently we don't know what happened to Blind Bartimaeus; maybe he founded a mission to the sighted.

October 28: Cultural Literacy; Whose Culture?

The May 23, 2011 *Psychology Today* has a short test on cultural literacy. You're culturally literate if you know the meaning of: absolute zero, Alamo, Billy the Kid, Carpetbagger, El Greco, Fau*st*, gamma rays, the Homestead Act, Iago, Icarus, Jazz, lame duck, manna from heaven, nom de plume, penis envy, rococo, sea legs, tabula rasa,
Valhalla, Battle of Waterloo and Zeitgeist. Of course it depends on whose culture you're talking about. This would seem to be the culture of a liberal arts-educated white American.

October 29: Yates and Adversity

Today I attended the second lecture at the library about Yates, and I gave a talk at the Catholic student club at church about living with adversity. I cannot imagine showing up for a talk as a student to hear someone three times my age talk about adversity, but twenty students did. I discussed a wide range of points including its being okay to be angry at God; Job, St. Paul and Jesus asked to reason with God or let this cup pass them by. I suggested it was okay to occasionally have a pity party for yourself. I talked about balancing, giving, and taking help. For praying when you don't feel like it, I'm a fan of just showing up for your time with God and letting it happen. When helping others, I try to remember that God gave us two ears and one mouth, and I should use them accordingly. One gal had a light bulb go on when I talked about life being more like baseball than academics, in that if you hit one ball out of three, you're good, as opposed to having to get 90% to get an "A". Of course I told a couple dog stories and several students wanted to pet Luna because they miss their dogs at home. They had no questions. They were at least grateful for the homemade brownies a parishioner had provided. I wonder what was accomplished, but at least I showed up and swung at the topic.

October 30: Garlyn

Grief comes in waves when retiring and losing a Seeing Eye dog. The first wave is when you have to make the retirement decision; the second is when you actually do the retirement, and the third is when the animal dies. Today I found out that Garlyn, who is eleven and has been retired about six years, has advanced kidney failure. Her euthanasia will come soon. She hadn't been eating well lately, and when I lay by her last Friday night to try to sense what was ailing her, I could feel that she was running out of energy, and removing herself from this world. She has always been one to keep her own counsel and make her own decisions, but remained a loving, watchful presence in the world. Now she is going inward to get ready for her next journey. In some ways Luna is like her, reaching out when she chooses, and I've told her I hope she becomes wise like Garlyn someday. I'll get someone to come over and play with Luna while I go to be with Garlyn when she crosses the rainbow bridge. Garlyn exemplifies what Mary Oliver said in her poem "For I Will Consider my Dog Percy" "For he came to me impaired and therefore certain of short life, yet thoroughly rejoiced in each day. For when he came upon mud he splashed through it. … For when he sniffed it was as if he were being pleased by every part of the world."

October 31: Halloween

Halloween (with its supernatural blending of the world of the living and the world of the dead) is based on a Celtic holiday called Samhain. The festival marked the start of winter, and the last stage of the harvest, the slaughtering of animals. It was believed that the dark of winter allowed the spirits of the dead to transgress the borders of death and haunt the living. The dark of the upcoming winter season was seen as positive in some ways, like a time for seeds to germinate in the earth. Dark and light, good and evil, all are present.

At the Red Hat Halloween party I attended the usual devils, beauties, and even a nun were present. But the cleverest costume was "Five Shades of Gray" in homage to the *Fifty Shades of Gray* book phenomenon. Luna and I went as mother and daughter; I had pumpkins on my shirt, she had them on a neckerchief. There was a wonderful potluck as usual. The mixture of candy corn and peanuts for dessert was amazing. It's so much better than either item alone.

$$\mathbb{D}$$

November 1: Tips for the Sighted

To celebrate October as Blindness Awareness Month, I asked several LISTSERVS and friends to give their best tips for sighted people when around a blind person. Today I compiled and distributed them.

Best Advice for the Sighted When around a Blind or Visually Impaired Person

Treat Me Like an Adult. Please don't talk to me like I'm a child.
—Barbara; Spartanburg, South Carolina

If you're aware that a blind person is in need of a regular ride to school, church or some other regularly scheduled event feel free to say yes if you can commit to helping out with transportation. If you can't commit to helping most of the time either introduce the blind person to someone you know who lives some place that is on the way to the event or simply leave the situation alone.
—Chris, 26; Everett, Washington

Please don't grab me, especially the arm that has my cane in it.
—Yvonne, 48; Pennsylvania

Do _not Grab a person's arm; ask if the person needs help.
—Eric C.

Ask me if I need help rather than assume. Listen to my answer rather than follow your anxious agenda. We may accidentally hit your shoes with our cane, but we don't bite.
—Ericka; Kenosha, Wisconsin

Never go up to a blind person and say Guess who this is! Please, all sighted people, say the person's name when speaking to them in a crowd, such as, "Hello Nola, glad to see you at this concert, I am Sarah, and we met at church."
—Nola M.

Say "bye" when leaving a room or conversation. That way we know you're gone!
—Kathie; Wisconsin

Use the face of the clock when indicating the placement of food on a blind person's plate— potatoes at nine, etc.
—Claire; Texas

Ask before you pet a dog guide in order to not distract the working dog.
—Claire; Texas (many people submitted this)

All blind people are different. They desire help in different ways. Don't stress
if someone is offended by your asking if he or she needs help. It's not your problem,
you tried.
—David F.; Louisiana

Blind persons like to participate in all kinds of activities so never rule a blind
person out because you think they cannot participate.—Ask!
—Claire; Texas

You get extra credit if you tell us interesting points in the environment like a "wet paint" sign or that there are treats in the break room for so and so's birthday.
—Kathie; Wisconsin

November 2: Guilty Pleasures

There's a novel titled *Guilty Pleasures* and a Wikipedia article about the concept, so clearly its worth considering. If you define it as things you shouldn't like but do, I'm not sure I have any because I don't tell myself I shouldn't unless it's truly bad for me or others. Maybe silly pleasures would be a better term for me. In that case, the following come to mind: Oreos with double filling, really bad thrillers that are just bang-bang-good-guy-knocks-off-bad-guy books, hiring someone to clean my house once a month, listening to an upper class British accent saying anything, re-gifting when it works well, and nestling into bed with clean sheets right out of the dryer.

For Luna lying in the sun or by a warm air vent might qualify but there's no guilt; trying to get me to chase her when she's grabbed something she shouldn't have comes closer. She knows it's wrong, but it's so much fun! I guess not only humans have guilty pleasures.

November 3: Why I Do It

Today is another pet food and supplies delivery, seven years and counting. When I got my first guide dog, I was living on a graduate student's salary and sometimes wasn't sure if I'd get a ride to the store to get dog food. Luckily I always did. As Samuel Johnson put it, "those who do not feel pain seldom think that it is felt." It's the same reason I'll go testify for five hot meals a week for Park Towers residents at the County Board budget hearings in a couple weeks. I know what it's like to try to figure out what I have that I can cook to make a presentable meal for friends when it's been too long between shopping trips. I'm lucky to have friends who would pick up something for me, but I save that for needs like dog food or toilet paper.

November 4: Getting the News

Every day or so I get Inclusion Daily Express by e-mail and I'm always impressed with the aggregating of disability news that the editor Dave Reynolds has done. He's been doing it for about fifteen years and manages to catch up with good coverage on a wide variety of disability issues. I haven't found anything like it about issues facing us elders yet. *New York Times* "Aging Well" blog covers some, and AARP covers legislation well. I guess I'm looking for a *Reader's Digest* section of "News You Can Use" on Aging. I don't want to take on that project, but I wish someone would.

November 5: Another Age Well Book

Today I skimmed *The Hourglass Solution: A Boomer's Guide to the Rest of Your Life* by Paula Forman and Jeff Johnson.

Seventy-five million baby boomers are finding themselves bound by habits and pursuits started many years ago. For a large percentage of those boomers, significant aspects of their lives no longer satisfy. *The Hourglass Solution* provides a proactive
and pragmatic way to lead a better life after fifty. Johnson and Forman evaluate the
life narrative through the lens of an hourglass-proposing that those in early adulthood
are at the top of the hourglass, able to select from many options, while those in
middle age are in the hourglass's neck, constrained by the choices they made earlier
in their lives. *The Hourglass Solution* explains how those approaching their fifties
(and beyond) can still find a wealth of opportunity by recognizing and pursuing new
directions, free from the restrictions imposed by an earlier choice. Like Gail Sheehy's *Passages* before it, *The Hourglass Solution* can enlighten and inspire a generation of readers to regain control over their lives and well-being.

November 6: Living the Butterfly Effect Every Day

I woke up to slushy snowfall, the first of the season, and a day I didn't want to do. I guest lectured a class, voted, was interviewed by a student journalist, and went to be at Garlyn's euthanasia. As I was napping to escape the day, a friend called to worry about a county board budget item that I care deeply about too. I truly didn't want to talk about it, or anything. I know according to Andy Andrew's *The Butterfly Effect* and many other wise peoples' thinking everything you do does matter. I guess, ideally I would have said, "I'm having a bad day; can I call you tomorrow?" Instead I reluctantly talked and when she said she'd call again tomorrow, I agreed about as reluctantly as one could agree. Everything got done that needed to, but not necessarily graciously. What do you call that effect?

November 7: Getting Ready to do Battle

Healthy discontent is the prelude to progress.
-Mahatma Gandhi

Today I spent the day writing testimony and politicking. A county and federally-funded hot meal site at an apartment building for low-income disabled and elderly people is heading toward cutting hot meals from five days a week to four. That's unacceptable to me. So I'll testify and I think some of the residents will too. I will say:

> I'm Katherine Schneider and I live in Sue Miller's district. I do not live in Park Towers but have been there every month for the last seven years to deliver pet food and supplies through the Eau Claire County Humane Association's We All Love Our Pets program. I've gotten to know many people in the Park Towers community. It is a community—gossipy small town sometimes; a very caring community often.
>
> I serve on the Aging and Disability Resource Center. When I heard we might have to cut one meal a week at Park Towers I was horrified. What if that was my mom who was going to go from five hot meals a week to four!
>
> When you live on $781 per month as many Park Towers residents do, your budget is tight. If you need to take para-transit to get to and from the Community Table for a free meal, it costs $6.00. That's almost twice as much, and much harder to arrange if you're frail and/or elderly than eating at Park Towers. Unless it's one hundred degrees and our air-conditioning is broken, I would guess most of us consider a hot meal every day as just part of life. We provide this to our jail inmates.
>
> The congregate meal site at Park Towers serves two purposes: hot nutritious meals and community socialization. A resident I know who struggles with depression says that eating the meal and seeing her friends there gives her the get up and go to get out of her apartment at least once a day. Isolation, depression, illness, and hospitalization costs society more in the long run than this kind of meal program.

Please give the ADRC a $10,000 add back to fund the Park Towers congregate meal site five days per week as it is now.

November 8: It'll be an Interesting Ride

James Hillman says in *The Force of Character*, aging "is necessary to the human condition, intended by the soul. The older we become, the more our true natures emerge. Thus the final years have a very important purpose: the fulfillment and confirmation of one's character." Old people serve as ancestors, models for the young and bearers of a society's cultural memories.

As a Wisconsin politician said she didn't want to make history as the first openly gay U.S. Senator but wanted to make a difference. I know I have a passion to make the lives of people with disabilities better. I wonder how this will express itself as I continue occupying aging. *Tales from Rhapsody Home* by John Gould is a great example of somebody who did just that in an assisted living facility.

November 9: New Stage of Life

Marc Freedman the CEO of online magazine Encore has renamed retirement the encore stage of life. As he says: "we have the time and energy to live a legacy, instead of just leaving one." Today I did both. I'm starting to organize my end-of-year contributions to charities and continuing to politic for five days of hot meals per week at the Park Towers apartment. One of the charities I like to give to is Heifer International. You can give a goat, a flock of chickens, a hive of bees, or a variety of other animals to people in developing countries. I think they may have been one of the first groups to piece out what small contributions will buy; now I notice a lot of charities doing it. Heifer has gone a little crazy with it; such as their Peace on Earth package for $850. Needless to say I didn't buy that one. I'll buy a hive of bees and a flock of chickens. I'll let people on my Christmas card list know that because they get a Christmas letter e-mailed to them, or sent without a card, the money saved was used to buy the flock and the hive. I e-mailed the two friends I exchange charities with, and asked if they want to do it again this year. For those of us who have everything, a charity donation plus a plate of cookies or a jar of salsa is wonderful. I finished the day by reading some of Angie Arrien's meditations for the second half of life.

November 10: Gearing up for a Discussion of my Memoir

Next Sunday I've been asked to lead a discussion of my memoir, *To the Left of Inspiration*, on an online site mostly frequented by blind people.

I'll talk about why I wrote the memoir, to let people know they're not alone, to give a few tricks of the trade and to educate people without the disability. If asked, I've made a list of my top ten disability memoirs (excluding mine of course). I like them because they talk honestly about daily lived reality, neither being "I triumphed over," or "woe is me," kinds of books. Then I'll talk a bit about the hard parts of the endeavor of writing a memoir such as figuring out how much information is too much, and how to handle family secrets when family members are still living which was challenging for me. So was getting the memoir published.

I've come up with the following discussion questions:

Do you read memoirs? If so, what do you look for in them?

What are some of your favorite memoirs and why?

Do you read disability memoirs? If so, why and what do you look for in them?

If you read my memoir, what did you want more of and what did you want less of in it?

November 11: The Etiquette of Illness

The Etiquette of Illness: What To Say When You Can't Find The Words by Susan Halpern is a great book. It covers talking to children about illness, being around people with chronic illnesses, and what to do when death approaches. But like every advice book it speaks in generalities and acknowledges that each situation is different.

Particularly with chronic illnesses and disabilities, I've noticed people consistently saying a few things that are unhelpful and may even be harmful. "You look so good" although meant to be encouraging can be heard as "quit your whining." "I know somebody who had just what you have and they ate six tons of broccoli and now they're better."

Maybe that would help and maybe it wouldn't! "Maybe it's stress; just relax." So should I feel guilty for causing this? Can I just relax and get over it, now that you've told me to relax? "God must have a reason for giving you this cross to bear." That's bad theology and tends to make one hate God.

I'm struggling with how hopeful to be as I talk to my friend with cancer. I know that my job is to listen and to encourage, but what I read about her prognosis is not encouraging. When she talks about getting better, is that because she believes it or is she talking to cheer the rest of us up? I focus on daily events and hopes for family members' visits next week. I'll wait for an opportunity to talk about the big picture and both hope and fear that it comes soon.

I'll offer to cook for the onslaught of relatives so I can do something concrete to help.

November 12: Single and Sick

Either flu or food poisoning got a hold of me today and I spent 12 hours trying to figure out which end to point toward the toilet. The last time I was that sick I was visiting family, which I think is harder. Trying to talk to anyone civilly is too much for me when I'm that sick. The hard parts are taking care of Luna and having the energy to get up and open a bottle of soda. Luna figured out quickly to stay out of my way as I dashed to the john, but stayed closer than usual. She checked on me but wasn't a pest—good nursing skills. I did worry a little when I was having bad chills if I'd be aware enough to know if I needed to go to a doctor. Luckily, the chills passed after a couple hours with a heating pad. I hope I was polite to the callers I had. I do remember saying to my nephew's wife, "I've got to go now" —but didn't elaborate about the urgency of that sentence.

November 13: World Kindness Day and County Board Testimony

In honor of World Kindness Day I tried extra hard to speak kindly to everyone I encountered. It's a good thing this is only one day a year!

I testified at the County Board budget hearing. There were large groups testifying for the drug courts and for the coordination team that works with at risk kids. There was one man who talked about the Mexican Mafia and several other subjects in his three minutes before asking for his property to be rezoned. Our team of three, one resident of Park Towers and two of us concerned citizens made a good showing I think. The Park Towers resident was even interviewed afterwards by a local newspaper reporter. I ended the day by talking with a kind friend who is just home from the hospital again after much cancer treatment. It's easy to be kind to kind people!

November 14: Being Around People with Alzheimer's

As I age, I spend more time around friends who are part of the twelve million Americans living with Alzheimer's. I used to actively avoid these encounters. Doing lunches with a dear friend as he traveled the first few steps down the road to Alzheimer's helped me get more comfortable with it. So did reading *Losing My Mind* by Thomas Debaggio. His memoir of early Alzheimer's helped me understand what it felt like to this sensitive intelligent man.

Today I was practicing what I've learned and it went well. It was just a simple meal shared with friends, one of whom is developing dementia. The conversation was light, we laughed about our animals and I didn't pitch a fit about the person with dementia feeding my dog. It wasn't that much and I don't know of any allergies, so why fight. I need to remind myself Keep it Light!

News Flash: We got the ten thousand bucks from the County Board so Park Towers will have hot meals five days a week. A board member told me it was mainly because of the testimony of Park Towers residents, family members, and me. Yes!

November 15: Give Me Patience and Give it to Me Now!

Have courage for the great sorrows of life, and patience for the small ones. When
you have laboriously accomplished your daily tasks, go to sleep in peace. God is awake.
—Victor Hugo

Even though yesterday's victory at Park Towers was on the front page of the paper and plans were moving forward to figure out how to make changes there so we won't have to go through this again next year, I spent most of the day going "grrr". Getting services to happen for my friend just home from the hospital that needs some physical therapy and home care was one project I was picking at. I finally talked again to the attorney from Disability Rights Wisconsin about the law change necessary for a secret ballot in state elections, six months after our first conversation and she reminded me changing laws was a slow process. Nothing had happened at her end in the intervening six months and I was prickly and impatient. We agreed she'd talk to a lawyer at the Government Accountability Board to find out why the law was the way it was and I could contact her back in three weeks if she hadn't contacted me. I don't care why the law is the way it is; I just want it changed. I do see her point that if we have their backing, things will go better.

November 16: Benefits of Being Sick

This week as I've lain around recovering from flu or food poisoning, I've found two benefits of being sick. I've thoroughly enjoyed the breadth of programs on satellite radio and I've planned my next steps in four projects. I didn't feel up to reading so turned on BBC or other public radio streams on XM radio and would listen, fall asleep, wake, hear another new idea and drift off again. Then there are two classical channels if I just wanted music. Of course my Wisconsin Public Radio is usually on when I'm up and about, but XM is conveniently located by the bed, another reason to stay in bed a little longer.

I noticed as I was project planning that time flat on my back gave time for the plans to lie fallow and then get tweaked a bit and then rest some more. Each one got more joyful as time went on. Lying around can be amazingly productive.

November 17: Toxic vs. Transformative Charity

As I continue ruminating about what I want to share with the Women's Giving Circle from the perspective of someone who is both the recipient and the giver of philanthropy, I've been challenged by Robert Lupton's *Toxic Charity*. In it, Lupton urges individuals, churches, and organizations to step away from "feel good" spontaneous, often destructive acts of compassion toward thoughtful paths to community development.

He delivers proven strategies for moving from toxic charity to transformative charity. Proposing a powerful "Oath for Compassionate Service" and spotlighting real-life examples of people serving not just with their hearts but with proven strategies and tested tactics, Lupton offers tools and inspiration we need to develop healthy, community-driven programs that produce deep, measurable, and lasting change. People who volunteer or donate to charity need to wrestle with this book. I'm wrestling, particularly with regard to my We All Love our Pets program. The same people will have the same needs as long as they live and are pet owners. In that sense, nothing is transformed by our charity. Animals are just fed. To me (and I'm sure to them), it's worthwhile.

November 18: Being Appreciated Is Humbling

Today I led a book discussion online about my memoir on a website for blind people called Accessible World. I'd read several recent blindness memoirs and prepared questions, but was nervous about the feedback from my peers. Even though it's my memoir and I know it's true, I don't know how universal the experiences are and I don't know how my tone comes across. For the dozen people who showed up, apparently many experiences were similar and the tone was the right mix of humor, pain and transcendence. My focus on interdependence rather than a rigid independence was valued by several speakers. We talked a bit about the impact of additional disabilities as we age (which several of us are doing) and people's reactions to them. We agreed a lot of work remains to be done in educating professionals in the aging field. A new disability impacts someone's life differently than a lifelong disability does. Stories were told and laughs were shared. When I asked who was writing the next memoir, several people said they had stories to tell, but no time. I hope they do write their stories down because we need more true, not "walk on water" memoirs.

November 19: Lincoln and Me

Lincoln gave the Gettysburg address on this date in 1863. This two-minute speech: a model of brevity and a profound statement of what the United States stands for.

Upon request from Wisconsin Public Radio I created a one-minute testimonial for them today. In one minute I managed to list or describe ten programs and how they impact my life. We also recorded a couple of "nat sounds" to go in the background: my screen reader reading the daily program notes and e-mail and the sound of me Brailling. It will be interesting to hear what other board members come up with.

The other highlight of the day was shopping at a locally owned bookstore where the owner could find and recommend the perfect book for those hard to buy for people on my list. I bought a book of nature photographs from Minnesota for retired biologists and a book on the solar system with wonderful pictures for a science-minded young great nephew. I do love Amazon because I can shop online and browse by myself, but a real bookstore is wonderful too. That's my day— as Lincoln said "I walk slowly, but I never walk backward."

November 20: Prayer

Novelist and memoirist Anne Lamott has written a new book on prayer, *Help, Thanks, Wow*! To which I'd add "sorry."

Whether reading Lamott or *How I Pray, Praying Naked, Prayers of the Cosmos* or *Centering Prayer* (all of which I have enjoyed recently), I'm reminded there are many ways to pray, but you have to do it! Don't worry about doing it right and don't look for quick results, just listen and talk with God and the rest will work itself out. When I pray about a troubled relationship, my heart softens and new ideas of what I can do differently may bubble up. I used to think prayer would change that other person, and maybe it will, but it sure changes me.

November 21: Stop Day

"Stop day," is what author Matthew Sleeth calls the Sabbath in his new book *24/6*. I'm as guilty as the next person for working on Sunday. I try not to buy things unless I absolutely have to, hoping that stores could be closed and workers home with their families that day.

I truly think Thanksgiving ought to be a Stop Day. Yes I've called out a plumber when my garbage disposal choked on potato skins and I had a sink full of dishes and a house full of people. I think to have Black Friday starting Thanksgiving afternoon is just too much. There are online petitions for the big box stores to not do this, but its set to happen tomorrow. Some of us won't buy then, but I'll bet not enough to make a business difference.

I think *24/6* also applies to us retired people. When you don't work for pay it's easy to let projects like finishing manuscripts, getting ready for meetings, and keeping up with e-mail take way too much time. I need to declare mini Sabbaths if I'm not willing to take a whole day of rest.

One tip from the book may help. Take the phrase: "Be still, and know that I am God" (Psalm 46:10) Recite and breathe. Say it again, subtracting one word each time. At the end, just be.

November 22: Thanksgiving
Who does not thank for little will not thank for much. - Estonian proverb.

A Vietnamese proverb says, "When eating a fruit, think of the person who planted the tree." Some of the tree planters I'm particularly grateful to today are:
the people who raised, trained and paid for Luna; the people who work on holidays so the rest of us can eat drink and be merry the people who invented screen reading technology so I can read newspapers, e-mail, download a book and start reading it immediately;
the friends who enrich my life; and the Creator who gave me a beautiful world and senses with which to enjoy it.

November 23: Hired as an Elf
My friend who teaches blind and visually-impaired kids loved the print/braille books I'd gotten for her students and needed two more. I forwarded information to her about kids getting a print/braille letter from Santa. To simplify things, I'm going to do that, with my elf student worker's able assistance of course. Friends agreed to read my draft letter and give feedback. Never having seen such a letter, I want to get it right. I'd hate to be fired from elfhood! I bought fuzzy Christmas stickers for decorating the letters. So far my friends are no help about what Santa would write, tending to give me *Mad Magazine* kinds of suggestions. If you want a book full of those read *Santa Responds: He's Had Enough*.

November 24: Luna Helps me Read Scripture at Mass for the First Time
Today I read Scripture at Mass for the first time with Luna. This involves marching in with the assistant minister, followed by the priest during the opening hymn. As we walked to the front the priest got too close to Luna's rear for her comfort. She turned her head around and gave him the "shame on you for crowding me," look I hadn't seen

her give anyone since training. She was still walking forward, so I didn't correct her, just smiled to myself knowing what she was thinking. Like all of my dogs she enjoyed the fact that we would leave the church first at the end of the service.

Earlier in the day, I got a pine wreath for my mailbox. With temperatures in the twenties and thirties, it is starting to feel like Christmas is coming. I talked to Fran's new mom who has been in the hospital a couple times lately. I wanted to know if Fran was a burden and she said no. I also wanted her to know that I'd be glad to keep Fran while she rehabs from having her second knee replacement. After I reassured her that I wasn't going to grab Fran back and keep her, she said she'd truly consider my offer. Fran is well loved, that's for sure - another resolution of a situation to be thankful for.

November 25: There's a Little Carnegie in All of Us

Today is Andrew Carnegie's birthday. Carnegie is not just a name on 2,800 libraries that he endowed. He was a philanthropist to many cultural, educational and scientific institutions. He grew up poor and made his fortune in the steel industry. Critics can point out flaws in how he made his money, which is where I think he's similar to each of us. He was no saint, but he did some great things. I've appreciated going to many Carnegie libraries in my life. Think about that next time you're considering whether to attempt a good deed. Will the world be better off if you do this deed, even though it may not be done perfectly or with totally pure motives?

November 26: Dreams

At first dreams seem impossible, then improbable, then inevitable. - Christopher Reeve

Charles Schulz, the creator of *Peanuts* was born today. He had a tough time in school and his cartoons didn't make it into the school yearbook. He didn't get the girl he wanted. But his dream was to cartoon and at its height *Peanuts* was syndicated in 2,500 newspapers.

I've achieved fulfillment of many of my dreams, from swimming with dolphins to publishing two books. I've founded a children's book award, and a disability journalism award. These awards helped me realize my dream of better media coverage for disability issues.

To me the hardest part of the process is making the dream specific. A child at one of my school talks asked me what one wish or dream I had. I answered that I wished people in the world had enough to eat and that there was peace. That's two not one wish. Before I can do anything about it, I'll have to narrow it down a lot. But, the process starts with the dream.

November 27: Seeing Fran Again

Today a friend of mine, Luna, and I took lunch to Rae's. Luna got to meet Fran. Fran did the expected barking at Luna, and went crazy over her friend Marge. She made it clear that Rae shouldn't show interest in Luna. Luna wisely retired to the background and played with one of Fran's toys. By the end of the visit Luna and Fran were near each other and keeping to themselves. I invited Fran and Rae to help with Dogs in the Library next month. They eagerly accepted. All in all it was a delightful luncheon. We also got to meet a couple of Rae's friends who are animal nuts like Marge and me. Fran now has every educational toy for dogs that I've ever heard of. As smart as she is, she figured the toys out instantly. She looks healthy, happy and bossy and Rae clearly treasures her. Luna is resting up after a little reassurance that she is number one at my house. My heart is happy.

November 28: I and Thou

Today I went to a new study group at church on peace and justice. We're reading *Justice Rising* by Fr. John Heagle.

The first bit talked about treating others with respect. We should aim to have an I-thou relationship with them as Martin Buber would say, instead of an I-it relationship. My goal was to get through the meeting without treating anyone like an "it" when they were ignorant about my particular otherness, my disability. I gave myself extra credit if I could refrain from thinking "you stupid…"

I got full credit and so did others. I asked for some social action at church, an announcement from the pulpit that upon request Mardi Gras treats (served in our inaccessible basement) will be plated and brought up to accessible seats. Later I asked for personal "help" in that when these people see me at Mass, they should say hi and give their name. Time will tell how either of these requests is met, but I did voice them, and people agreed.

November 29: Traveling

I joined the twenty-four million Americans traveling during the holiday season. After having been thoroughly searched, including having my hands wiped and scanned for explosives, Luna and I flew to Chicago to visit the rest of the Schneider clan. As we taxied for takeoff, a mom read her child a Bible story book about the Armageddon and the end of the world. I thought about reassuring her that I had been checked for explosives, so we were good to go and would have a fine trip, but decided to just sit back and enjoy the flight.

November 30: Being a Good PANK

I found out that there's a name for what I am, a PANK, "professional aunt, no kids." We have the discretionary income to buy good presents, expose the nieces and nephews to culture, and hope to be a trusted adult that the kids can talk to.

I've loved watching my nephews grow and now raise their own kids. I've gotten to be part of both good times and bad. When they reach out voluntarily to visit or call, it's all worthwhile. I worry when I don't hear how a situation turns out. They may be getting old enough to realize that there is an art to caring for a PANK including updates and an occasional thank you. I think I'm ready for the visiting, entertaining and gifting part of being a PANK.
Jared Diamond in *The World Until Yesterday* talks about seniors in our culture needing to keep contributing. He mentions grand-parenting, but I guess I'll PANK.

☽

December 1: Good News

I'm reading *Major Pettigrew's Last Stand* by Helen Simonson for one of my book clubs. The gal who picked it chose it because it was a positive book. Although there's prejudice and other small-mindedness, good triumphs in the end. Mature adults were sometimes wise elders in the story. I started reading it thinking "not my kind of book," too sweet and simple and not enough trauma or dead bodies to be interesting. The characters interested me and I enjoyed myself in spite of myself.

I've begun reading parts of the *Huffington Post* and was pleased to see a part of it called "Good News." Of course in a recent issue there was one article in that section out of 167 total articles. I don't believe for a minute that's all the good news there was, but obviously good news doesn't sell as well as bad. An older friend often reminds me every day you wake up and are alive is a good day. That is good news.

December 2: Highlights of My Trip to Chicago

The trip to Chicago went well. Luna charmed the family's Dachshund and let him win at tug of war even though she outweighed him five to one. The whole family laughed a lot watching the two dogs play. Other highlights included: hosting a dinner at Red Lobster and a breakfast at a family restaurant for different parts of the tribe. a Presbyterian contemporary service done with loud rock versions of Advent songs like "Come Thou Long-Expected Jesus" and gluten-free communion bread was quite a change from my usual Mass at the Newman Center. Attending Addison Historical Society's Christmas potluck with plenty of good food and people sharing memories of Christmas past put me in the mood for this Christmas.

Luna and I talked to my great niece's second grade class. They wrote charming thank you notes. In hers, she called me a "great ant." I'd crawl to Chicago for that kind of compliment. A young family member with Asperger's wins the "aren't kids darling" story contest. I was outside with him giving his parents a break and he was telling me in great detail about all kinds of rocks as he found them in the garden. One, he told me, was coal. He further lectured me that if you put pressure on it, it would become a diamond. He then proceeded to stand on it for fifteen seconds and then looked at it. He was vexed it hadn't turned to a diamond yet. I know just how he feels! All in all, it was a good trip. When we got home, Luna ate and lay down to rest for three hours. It was tough work charming Dachshunds, but she did it!

December 3: International Day of Persons with Disabilities

I celebrated International Day of Persons with Disabilities in many ways. I called my pet food delivery customers, most of whom have disabilities. I enjoyed the freedom to read and write e-mail and surf the Internet. I also received home delivered books from the public library and walked freely with my Seeing Eye dog.

PRESIDENT'S PROCLAMATION FOR INTERNATIONAL DAY FOR PERSONS WITH DISABILITIES

Americans have always understood that each of us is entitled to a set of fundamental freedoms and protections under the law, and that when everyone gets a fair shot at opportunity, all of us do better. For more than two decades, our country has upheld those basic promises for persons with disabilities through the Americans with Disabilities Act — a sweeping civil rights bill that moved our Nation forward in the journey to equality for all. And from making health care more affordable to ensuring new technologies are accessible, we have continued to build on that progress, guided by the belief that equal access and equal opportunity are common principles that unite us as one Nation.

On the 20th International Day of Persons with Disabilities, we reaffirm that the struggle to ensure the rights of every person does not end at our borders, but extends to every country and every community. It continues for the woman who is at greater risk of abuse because of a disability and for the child who is denied the chance to get an education because of the way he was born. It goes on for the 1 billion people with disabilities worldwide who all too often cannot attend school, find work, access medical care, or receive fair treatment. These injustices are an affront to our shared humanity — which is why the United States has joined 153 other countries around the world in signing the Convention on the Rights of Persons with Disabilities, which calls on all nations to establish protections and liberties like those afforded under the Americans with Disabilities Act. While Americans with disabilities already enjoy these rights at home, they frequently face barriers when they travel, conduct business, study, or reside overseas. Ratifying the Convention in the Senate would reaffirm America's position as the global leader on disability rights and better position us to encourage progress toward inclusion, equal opportunity, full participation, independent living, and economic self-sufficiency for persons with disabilities worldwide.

We have come far in the long march to achieve equal opportunity for all. But even as we partner with countries across the globe in affirming universal human rights, we know our work will not be finished until the inherent dignity and worth of all persons with disabilities is guaranteed. Today, let us renew our commitment to meeting that challenge here in the United States, and let us redouble our efforts to build new paths to participation, empowerment, and progress around the world.

NOW, THEREFORE, I, BARACK OBAMA, President of the United States of America, by virtue of the authority vested in me by the Constitution and the laws of the United States, do hereby proclaim December 3, 2012, as International Day of Persons with Disabilities. I call on all Americans to observe this day with appropriate ceremonies, activities, and programs.

IN WITNESS WHEREOF, I have hereunto set my hand this third day of December, in the year of our Lord two thousand twelve, and of the Independence of the United States of America the two hundred and thirty-seventh.

BARACK OBAMA

December 4: Tis the Season for Gifts

According to an article in the *Wall Street Journal* about the science behind gifting by Sumathi Reddy research shows people prefer hinted-for gifts rather than "thoughtful" ones. I'm doing okay with my gifts so far. Thoughtful doesn't count as much as giving what people want. The fact I give money to several relatives is fine. Re-gifting is okay with eighty percent of people, and a quarter admits to having done it within the last year. I certainly am among them. I have trouble knowing what's out there because there are no ads in Braille magazines and I don't watch television. When someone gives me something cute but unneeded, I often re-gift. I don't have to hang my head. Luckily how much you spend doesn't seem to matter either. It's kind of hectic figuring out who gets what and will I have it by the time I see them in the run up to Christmas. It always seems to work out. I haven't thought of the perfect gift for my first Christmas with Luna, but it may well be a bath.

December 5: I'd Better Grow up Soon

Today I went to a congregate meal site for lunch to ask the diners what we could do to make the meal more appealing to fellow residents of the building. Luckily they were serving tuna and noodles so I could eat the main dish. There were overcooked peapods and Jell-O with canned fruit cocktail in it which was okay. There were also canned pears which I won't eat on a dare. Milk and bread rounded out the meal. If I ever land in a facility where I'm bound to eat their food, I'll have real problems remaining a vegetarian. Most don't offer that option. I may have to deal with the "do you want to eat or don't you," being my choices rather than, "what would you like?" I'll need to use my "be gracious" skills every day, three times a day. They were taxed to the max at Seeing Eye for eighteen days. Today I could feel my nice muscles protesting their lack of use, and their dislike of getting back in shape, and it was only for two hours. I hope it doesn't happen any time soon. I'm not ready!

December 6: St. Nick and Me

St. Nicholas was a fourth-century bishop of Myra, in southern Turkey whose humility and generosity were legendary. Santa Claus came out of this tradition. It seems appropriate that today I'm Brailling letters to three blind kids who wrote their wishes to Santa Claus. Santa is happy to be visiting them and thinks they will like his presents, but he is not making specific promises.

I was given a gift today of a gentle way to say to a friend that she'd said way too much in a situation. My initial angry thoughts of "I'm mad, that's the last time I tell you anything" moderated with prayer to, "It sounds like we both learned something. I learned to tell you how much you can share, and you learned that sometimes less is better."

Thanks for the present, St. Nick.

December 7: There's a Word for It

I'm fascinated by words, word games, and puns. This time of year I enjoy learning what words *Oxford English Dictionary* editors and other luminaries have chosen as words for the year. Some nominees for words of 2012 are: fiscal cliff, Ganghnam Style, YOLO, frankenstorm and superstorm. I had to look up "YOLO" texting for "you only live once." *Oxford American Dictionary* says the word of 2012 is "GIF." *Dictionary.com* says it should be "bluster". Oxford University Press has chosen an apt Word of the Year: "omnishambles." It is defined as, "a situation that has been comprehensively mismanaged, characterized by a string of blunders and miscalculations."

I guess I'll choose YOLO because this year has reminded me many times of the truth of that saying.

December 8: Getting Ready for Next Year's Lobbying

Feb. 5, 2013 will be the next Library Legislative Day in Wisconsin. I will get a ride to Madison with local public library advocates and remind legislators that funding for the Wisconsin Talking Book and Braille Library and NFB Newsline is vital. People from the Wisconsin Library Association help with talking points, making legislator appointments and making everyone feel comfortable, whether you're new to lobbying or an old pro. I always take cookies for legislators and their staffs. With a cute dog by my side, we're remembered whether or not our talking points are.

December 9: Luna Becomes an Adult

Today we had five inches of snow. Since Luna was trained in the spring and summer, we have to begin working on snow and ice skills.

Our first work in snow, walking around the block, went well. Conditions were ideal for working on staying on the sidewalk even if it's not shoveled. I use the word "path" to ask for that. I even had a piece of meat to give her as a reward when we got home safe. When I took her out for a bathroom break, she wanted to burrow and jump around. I had to tell her those days were over except when she's in a fenced yard. It's time to be an adult. It made me sad, but she seemed to accept it.

December 10: Progress not Perfection

A thought for the day from a well-respected recovery organization kept me struggling all day. "Progress not perfection" it said. But I wanted to shovel my sidewalks perfectly after our fifteen inch snow. Part of this is in my control, but at the edges of my property I don't know when to stop shoveling until my neighbors shovel. They were in no rush to do so.

Tomorrow is the Red Hat Christmas party and I had heard the game we were going to play depended on being able to see colors. I wanted to figure out the perfect solution without even knowing the rules. It is just a game, but I felt one down and mad about being in this spot at a Christmas party.

Then I fussed in my mind about not having the perfect presents for upcoming get togethers with friends. I don't get invites to go window shopping, where of course I'd spot the perfect present at the perfect price! What do you mean Christmas is about the presence of God on earth, not presents?

I talked to a friend who is feeling badly because she has to wear braces on both legs and it'll never get better for her. Progress for both of us clearly would be in the area of gracious acceptance, but I at least wasn't in the mood.

I could see progress in Luna's work in snow. But then she got busy showing me she wasn't perfect by grabbing a piece of paper and running around like a wild woman wanting me to chase her. Grrrr! I was glad when the end of the day came and I could say, "I'll think about progress not perfection another day."

December 11: A Friend Died

This morning I got word that a dear friend lost her battle with cancer. I spent a good bit of the day notifying people and organizations of her death and trying to figure out what I could do to be useful to out of town children who will arrive soon. Note to self: make a list and keep it with my important papers of who should be notified in case of my death.

December 12: Our Lady of Guadalupe

On this day in 1531, the Virgin Mary appeared to a Native American Christian convert on a hilltop outside of what is now Mexico City. The image she left imprinted on his cloak has puzzled scientists for centuries, but her message of love, unity, and hope has attracted millions to a devotion to Our Lady of Guadalupe. I like this feast day because it reminds me that God takes an interest in and appears to the poor and marginalized not just the important people in society. May I notice how and who God uses to speak to me today.

December 13: St. Lucy and Me

Today is the Feast of St. Lucy, the patron saint of blindness. Saint Lucy was a Sicilian maiden who suffered martyrdom during the early persecution of the Church, perhaps around the year 308. After dreadful tortures, she died for her faith by having a sword driven through her throat. Saint Lucy is often portrayed holding a plate upon which is two eyes.

Legend has it that, in order to escape the approaches of a young noble who was attracted by the beauty of her eyes, she had them cut out. But God, pleased with her life of virtue and honor, later restored her sight. I guess I shouldn't be so choosy, but I'd rather have a saint like Joan of Arc who would battle ignorance about blindness and the capabilities of blind people. Or even St. Francis Xavier who traveled the world educating people would be preferable to St. Lucy to me. The Catholic free library for books in alternate format is named after him. Voluntary blindness to avoid being attractive to over-zealous suitors is not a common experience in the blindness community!

December 14: Christmas Carols

I love Christmas carols. Some of my favorites are "O Holy Night," "Go Tell it On the Mountain," and "I Heard the Bells on Christmas Day". Why the newer carols are not so memorable, I don't know.
Tonight I was at a Red Hat gathering and they had us singing Red Hat carols —news to me!
The following are some that we sang:
"Away in Our Purple," "In a Red and Purple Wonderland," and "We Are the Red Hat Ladies" (to the tune of Rudolph). The 12 Days of Christmas for Red Hats includes "Coot and Biddy Figurines" among the gifts.

December 15: Desperately Seeking an Interpreter

For my friend's memorial service next Friday, I volunteered to arrange a sign language interpreter because her son and his fiancé are deaf. The interpreter I know is busy at school that day, as are several others. One was interpreting medical appointments at that time. Another didn't like doing religious services. I thought about saying, "Please just cross your fingers and help me out," but didn't. Each one who said "no" heard my desperation and gave me other names. If I get a licensed one, the state will pay for funeral interpretation. At this point I don't care; all I need is someone who knows sign.

On the ninth call I scored, and she's even licensed! I made a few more calls and started the proper paperwork. I did send her the poems that will be read. It may take a bit of time to find the sign for "henceforth" and some other archaic words in the poems.

December 16: A Little Bit of Humor

I read another study today touting the benefits of laughter. Just like exercise it increases endorphins if you do enough of it. Somehow I've been low on it lately. Luckily, some supposedly genuine senior dating ads dropped into my inbox today. An example is,

"LONG-TERM COMMITMENT SOUGHT: Recent widow who has just buried fourth husband, looking for someone to round out a six-unit plot."

It made me think about running ads for blindness (like anybody would sign up). "Want to grope around public bathroom stalls looking for the toilet paper because it's never in the same spot—try blindness" or "Want to learn to be a neater person and put things in a consistent place so you can find your keys? Try blindness." "Tired of driving your kids around all the time? Try blindness and you can all use public transportation instead."

I'm sure other disability groups could offer their own ads. If I can't laugh, I guess I'd have to up my exercise routine to get more endorphins and that would be painful.

December 17: A Varied Day in Retirement

In addition to sundry house chores like emptying the dishwasher and dragging the garbage can through the snow to the curb today, I met with a mentee. Then I organized a cavalcade to bring two tons of boxes of kitty litter for the pet food and supply program to my garage. We'll receive the boxes of kitty litter Friday from the Petco Foundation. I have an idea for publicity to thank Petco, a photo of a stuffed cat sitting atop 134 thirty-pound buckets of kitty litter with a sign reading: "ECCHA's We All Love Our Pets program thanks Petco Foundation for donating two tons of kitty litter."

Today I had the blind graduate student over for breakfast and mentoring. She brought her youngest child, a babe of about three months. As we ate and chatted, the baby continually spit up. Some of it fell on Luna who promptly cleaned it up. This process was repeated several times during the meeting. Luckily when I got the chance to hold the babe, she did not spit up. I almost lost my appetite, which is a serious situation that rarely happens. I compare it with last Thursday when I was holding a black lab future Leader Dog of about equal heft. If he had released bodily fluids on me (which didn't happen) I wouldn't have missed a beat. To each her own, I guess.

In retirement my listening skills are employed in mentoring and my organizational skills in getting two tons of boxes of kitty litter from point A to point B. What an interesting life!

December 18: Just Because You Can See Doesn't Mean You Can See

A friend of mine coined this phrase when I was pestering her about not seeing something that was quite visible. A wonderful example happened this morning. I was at a business women's breakfast held by a local hospital. The company was good, the talk was inspiring, and the food smelled great. I was exploring my plate, first with my fork and later with my fingertips because I wasn't clear on some parts of it. There was a small sweet roll, some thin slices of melon, some sausages (which I removed for my non-vegetarian Seeing Eye dog to consume later), and what I figured was a scrambled egg mixture on top of a lettuce leaf. But what on earth was on top of it? I picked it up and tossed it aside, guessing it was an orchid or some such fancy thing. Afterwards I asked two friends what it was. One confirmed it was an orchid which she had not eaten. The other friend said, "I was hungry and I ate it all; I have no idea what I ate." I guess she *was* hungry! She had no bad effects, so orchids must be edible. It made me smile, knowing that she who could see had not noticed.

December 19: After Care-giving

About sixty-five million people in the U.S. are caregivers. Jane Heller, novelist and author of *You'd Better Not Die or I'll Kill You: A Caregiver's Survival Guide to Keeping You in Good Health and Good Spir-*

its, talks about caring for yourself while caring for others. *A Funny Thing Happened on My Way to the Dementia Ward: Memoir of a Male CNA* by Charles Schoenfeld shows the usefulness of humor in keeping sane as a caregiver.

Today I had lunch with two former caregivers. One is just starting to think about how to fill the time she no longer devotes to care-giving. The other is still a caregiver but in a more diffuse way; she's the informal activities director for the assisted-living facility where she resides. If one member of a couple there has Alzheimer's, she makes sure that person has a signed birthday card to give to their spouse. She donates her large print books to the library after reading them. She invites someone without close family to her Christmas lunch with friends. Both are a bit blue at the holiday season, but are giving care to the community anyway. Maybe that's part of how they care for themselves. I find both of them to be Impressive! As Churchill said, "We make a living by what we get, but we make a life by what we give."

December 20: Six Word Memoirs of Aging and Disability

Guide Dogs, Braille, Friends—Thanks God.

Slower? Yes, but much to savor.

Not paid work, but chosen work.

Friends are here and in Heaven.

Aches, pains, laughter, joy, maybe wisdom.

December 21: Life, Suffering, and a Memorial Service

Although the world is full of suffering, it is full also of the overcoming of it.   —Helen Keller

In *Pilate's Prisoner by* Edward Hays' Jesus ponders his existence. He does not see himself as a unique hero but instead in union with all fellow humans. We are all confronted by a mysterious universe where life is a gift defined by how fully and gratefully we live it instead of by our eagerness to escape it.

Today I went to a memorial service for a good friend who died of cancer. In addition to traditional scriptures of comfort like Psalm 23, she had chosen two poems: "Thanatopsis" and "Snowbound." Her PEO sisters, church members, and retired university colleagues showed up in good numbers to celebrate a life of teaching and gracious service to her community. The sign language interpreter kept up with the preacher (who had a South African accent), hymns, and poetry. She also accompanied deaf family members through condolences and lunch conversation. The day was cold and clear. I think my deceased friend would have appreciated the inclusive, quietly joyous celebration of life, and her life in particular.

December 22: Day After

Yesterday was the solstice, so days are getting longer. The day after my friend's memorial service, I talked to her husband and he was moving forward and seemed a bit less deep in his grief. I'm reminded of words from the carol they're playing, "You are the New Day":

> Like a breath I knew would come I reach for
> the new day
>
> Hope is my philosophy
> Just needs days in which to be
> Love of life means hope for me
> borne on a new day
>
> You are the new day

Late in the day someone called needing to know how to get groceries delivered to them —they're afraid of falling on the ice. Because of the life we celebrated yesterday and the Christmas season, I was a little nicer about saying "Sure I'll call them and tell them about the Bag Ladies, (two women who shop and deliver groceries.)" Somebody gave me a tacky Christmas gift, but I crafted a grateful e-mail that did not commit perjury. I know the New Day won't last, but that's the hope of the Christmas season that it will.

December 23: Humanlight

In addition to Christmas, Hanukkah, and Kwanzaa, secular humanists have added a new celebration to December's calendar— Humanlight. On or about December 23, candles are lit for reason, compassion, and hope. More power to them I say. It's not my primary holiday this time of year, but I'd be glad to celebrate it too. Happy Humanlight!

December 24: Christmas Reading

I'm a sucker for good contemporary Christmas stories. Sister Joan Chittister talked about celebrating the "call to begin once more the journey to human joy and holy meaning" at this time of year. To me a good Christmassy story has believable characters, a good plot, and shows the joy, peace, giving, and hope of the season. Of the four Christmas stories I read this year, *Merry Christmas Alex Cross* by James Patterson was the best. A detective foiled a robbery of a poor box at a church, solved a domestic standoff with less bloodshed than expected, and pulled off a miracle in an international terrorism scenario all during December 25. *The Christmas Box* by Richard Paul Evans was a bit too sweet, like the second piece of fudge after Christmas dinner. *This Year It Will Be Different and Other Stories* by Maeve Binchy had the well-drawn characters I love her books for, but somehow I don't want to hear about extramarital affairs in my Christmas reading. *The Christmas Wedding* (also by Patterson with a different co-author) had strong characters but not as much plot as I expect from him. Now I'm ready to go back to my usual assortment of memoirs, thrillers, and social science and religious nonfiction.

December 25: Favorite Christmas Things and Happenings

To serve is beautiful, but only if it is done with joy and a whole heart and a free mind.
—Pearl S. Buck

Many of my favorite things this Christmas were service-related, but some were just pure hedonistic joys. Favorites this year (starting with the hedonistic ones) included:
lolling around reading Christmassy books; having a beautiful pine wreath on my mailbox to smell every time I check for mail; tastes of the season like eggnog, gingerbread men, lefse, and cringle; and listening to light classical Christmas music on satellite radio.

I enjoyed many opportunities to serve my community. I made pet food and supply deliveries, including small presents for humans and pets. I got to be Santa and write Santa letters for blind kids. I gave a gift that really matters— blood—at a Red Cross blood drive. I hosted a Leader Dog puppy gathering. I got to hold a ten pound sleeping future Leader Dog and feel the love that the raisers pour into their charges every day. I organized gatherings ranging from a lunch we took to friends at an assisted living facility to a Scrabble game Christmas afternoon. A van load of four people and two dogs drove around while looking at Christmas lights, laughing, and telling stories.

I took Luna and a retired guide dog to be petted for Dogs in the Library for finals week.

I hosted a Hanukkah talk at Park Towers. I organized the cavalcade of boxes of kitty litter donated by Petco Foundation from their store to my garage.

I can't imagine how Christmas could have been improved.

December 26: Starting to Think about Next Year's Projects

Ben Franklin said, "Be always at war with your vices, at peace with your neighbors, and let each New Year find you a better man." Now that Christmas is over, except for celebrating with two sets of friends, I'm beginning to plan next year's projects. So far, three have announced themselves:

1.   Read the Bible from beginning to end. The accessible commentaries I found will help me book by book, but I couldn't find an accessible one that divides it up week by week. I guess I'll have to do the math myself!

2.   E-mail journalists who've written good articles about disability issues since July 1, suggesting they apply for the new disability journalism award I'm sponsoring through the National Center for Disability Journalism at the Walter Cronkite School of Journalism at Arizona State.

3.   Write an article or make a speech to philanthropists about philanthropy that feels good and empowers the recipient. As someone who has received charity as well as given it, I have something to say. My research will include skimming at least ten books I've found on philanthropy and getting feedback from other people who've been receivers of charity. I put it out on a very talkative LISTSERV and only three people responded to my questions. My questions included the following:

What can donors do to make it feel less icky to take charity?

When does it feel good to say thanks?

What would you tell philanthropists about charitable giving if you had the chance?

December 27: Today's Opportunity to Serve

Today a friend e-mailed as follows:

"I wonder if you have any ideas on what to do about an elevator problem. My grandma lives on the third floor of an apartment building downtown, and the elevator has been broken for three weeks, ever since there was a power surge. There are some people in the building who use walkers, so they are stuck. It is awfully hard on ninety-two -year-old Grandma too. The property manager seems to be dragging their (sic) feet. Now it is going to be four more weeks to get a part. Grandma has called the Eau Claire building inspector, Health Department, housing authority, and Public Works Department. They were all very nice and all called the property owner, but things haven't been speeded up at all. Do you have any ideas on anything else that could be done? We told Grandma to withhold her rent and try to get others in the building to do the same. Thought I'd ask you since you are a miracle worker."

I replied:

"I'm sorry your relative is having this problem. The ADA requires that accessibility features must be repaired promptly. I got more voice-mails, leave a message, etc. than one would believe, but as much as I can piece together, she'd be well within her rights to file an ADA complaint with the Department of Justice. To find out how to do that, call 800-949-4232.

Sometimes getting a lawyer to write a letter saying, 'We are going to do this if the problem is not resolved within a week,' and sending it return receipt requested makes people know you're serious. Then there's the personal approach of making an appointment with the head of the real estate company, taking a witness, and shaming them about 'what if it was your mother.' Another idea for the letter or conversation is requesting something like, 'Until the elevator is fixed, I want the property manager to come up once a day, bring my mail, and take down my trash.' That gives the company something they can do to make it better in the meantime and gives them some skin in the game. Of course I'd be glad to go with you if you decide on this route.

The Center for Independent Living 715-514-4200 (Eau Claire office), or 800-228-3287 (main office in Menomonie) may have other ideas. When I talked to a staff member at the Aging and Disability Resource Center at 715-839-4735, they thought my ideas were good and they will e-mail me back if they come up with something better. If you're comfortable telling me the address of the property, I'd be glad to call and speak to the owner or manager myself. I'm all for doing something today, because I think even fewer people will be at their desks tomorrow and through to January 2."

When I talked to the manager, it turned out they did have four hours of "gopher" service available for residents five days a week and residents could call their twenty-four hour number if they needed something done at another time. The manager thought the company building the new mother board for the elevator was doing their best and that nothing more could be done.

All I could think of would be for the resident to move to a motel for the duration, but to me that would be more disruptive than using the gopher service. I think they called the newspaper to see if they wanted to do a story. That's one thing that is really hard about having disabilities sometimes; the "reasonable accommodations" are not nearly as good, timely, or cheap as the mainstream way of doing things. It just stinks. Even when people are doing their best, it isn't good. I try to avoid filing a grievance, suing, and going to the newspaper unless I think the violator could do more if they really wanted to. But some people find those tactics useful just because it makes them feel heard and that helps. I sure wish I could make it better.

December 28: Families

Those who love you are not fooled by mistakes you have made or dark images you hold about yourself. They remember your beauty when you feel ugly; your wholeness when you are broken; your inno-

cence when you feel guilty; and your purpose when you are confused
—African saying

During this season of the year, there's lots of emphasis on family. When I was in college, I realized I could make honorary family members to add to my biological family. Now I'm thankful for natural, created, extended, and extraordinary family members I have. I had supper with a couple that I'm close to on a deep level of comfort, even though we don't gather often. Our Christmas celebration was muted because of our unacknowledged losses of friends. As we talked about next year, I quoted another friend's wish that there'd be "more smiles and less tears" and we toasted that sentiment. As I lose family members, I pray that I remain open to making new connections.

December 29: *The Purple Chair*
I was really taken with the story of Nina Sankovitch chronicled in *Tolstoy and The Purple Chair.* Her sister died of cancer, and she ran around like crazy for three years trying to live enough for both of them. Then she decided to sit still in a purple chair and read a book a day for a year. She looked to books for how to live with her sorrow and how to find her place in the world. She devoted about four hours a day to this in between taking care of her busy family.

Maybe my year of journaling has started me on a similar journey, but I feel a need to do more. Possibly the Bible in a year project will scratch that itch if my reading is contemplative, not just intellectual. My occupying of aging has just begun I can tell.

December 30: Luna and I after Four Months
When I first got Luna, she was polite and friendly enough, but I could just tell I wasn't seeing all of her. Of course this is natural and I knew when she and I got home we'd learn lots about each other.

Today she showed me another facet of her character and I'm thinking I may know almost all of her depths. A friend and I had enjoyed Christmas cookies that she brought and we went into the kitchen to get some tea. I commented on how much we trust Luna and how good she is. No problem. Two hours later, I'm working on the computer and hear noises in the dining room. When I run in Luna is eating a cookie. I check the plate, still on the table and still containing most of the cookies, but the saran wrap is gone and I panic that she's eaten it. I start groping around the floor and find the wrap all balled up but intact. I call Luna over and spend about thirty seconds telling her how bad she was to steal a cookie. She appears slightly repentant but then walks over, puts her face in mine, and gives a giant belch. I walk away to keep myself from laughing. Two minutes later she comes over to ask if I still love her. Most labs I know would pull the plate off the table and eat plate, cookies, and wrap all at once. To spend time pulling the wrap off and balling it up to me shows amazing forethought and possible prior experience.

After four months and her recent learning to work in snow and ice, I know she's smart and careful in her work, but her nose for food is strong. Clearly her planning skills are good too. I wonder what facet of her character she'll show me next.

December 31: Looking Back, Looking Forward
The years teach us much, which the days never knew
—Ralph Waldo Emerson

This year I learned a lot about walking beside the dying and the grieving. I've worked on disability issues in a variety of ways. I've met many good souls along the way. I experienced the blessing of friends who encouraged me onward when I didn't know if I could give my heart and soul to a new Seeing Eye dog again so soon. Occasionally, I could see growth in my tolerance for others' foibles. I savored the little daily joys that cost nothing and mean everything. I read a multitude of good books and had some wonderful laughs.

> For next year, I'll offer this Irish toast:
> "May the new year help to make us old.
> May the New Year bring summer in its wake."
> And join Jonathan Swift in wishing: "May you live all the days of your life."

Acknowledgments

My most profound thanks go to God and the two Seeing Eye dogs who led me through this year. I made it through the year chronicled here with the guidance of God and Fran and Luna. They did their bests and what I did with their guidance is for the reader to judge.

Thanks to Dr. Ruth Cronje and her spring 2013 English 307 class at the University of Wisconsin-Eau Claire for their initial editing of *Occupying Aging*. They treated me with care and respect and taught me much about the English language. This elder enjoyed learning from each of them. Special thanks to a special student in this class, Amanda Ponzio-Mouttaki who finished the editing. Polishing the manuscript with this intelligent and hard-working young woman, passionate about reaching across cultural divides of all kinds, renewed my confidence in those who will be occupying aging down the line.

Dogear Publishing describes themselves as"self-publishing that actually makes sense." Ray Robinson and his team at Dogear deliver on this promise and do so with grace and style. Thanks a million!

Thanks to you who have read *Occupying Aging*. If you have reactions to it, I'd love to hear from you. Please email me at schneiks@uwec.edu.

All the best.

Kathie

July 1, 2013

Recommended Reading

Agus, David. 2012. *The End of Illness*. New York: Free Press

Akhter, Ayad. 2012. *American Dervish*. New York: Little, Brown

Album, Mitch. 2012. *Time Keeper*. New York: Hyperion

Alexie, Sherman. 2007. *The absolutely true diary of a part-time Indian*. Little Brown Books for Young Readers

Alford, Henry. 2013. *Would it Kill You to Stop Doing That?* New York: Twelve

Ambrose, Jeanne. *Heartbreak Recovery Kitchen: Recipes and Remedies for Mending and*
Moving On. Handcrafted Words

Amen, Daniel. 2012. *Use Your Brain to Change Your Age*. New York: Crown Archetype

Amir, Nina. 2012. *How to Blog a Book*. Writer's Digest Books

Andrews, Andy. 2009. *The Butterfly Effect*. Naperville, Ill.: Simple Truths

Armstrong, Jeffery. 2010. *Spiritual Teachings of the Avatar*. Atria Books/Beyond Words

Arrien, Angeles. 1998. *The Second Half of Life*. Boulder, CO: Sounds True

Auster, Paul. 2012. *Winter Journal*. New York: Henry Holt and Co.

Barnes, Julian. 2011. *The Sense of an Ending*. New York: Alfred A. Knopf

Bartlett, Jennifer, al eds., 2011. *Beauty Is a Verb: The New Poetry of Disability*. Cinco
Puntos Press

Baucells, Manel. 2012. *Engineering Happiness : A New Approach for Building a Joyful Life*. Berkley: University of California Press

Beaton, M.C. 2010. *Agatha Raisin and the Vicious Vet*. London: Constable

Bianco, Margery. 2012. *The Velveteen Rabbit*. Kennebunkport, Me.: Appleseed Press

Binchy, Maeve. 1996. *This Year will be Different*. New York: Delacorte Press

Birchall, Cathy. 2012. *Touching the World*. High Wycombe: Panther

Bourgeault, Cynthia. 2004. *Centering Prayer*. Cowley Publications

Brees, Drew. 2010. *Coming Back Stronger*. Carol Stream, Ill.: Tyndale House Publishers

Brett, Regina. 2012. *Be the Miracle*. New York: Grand Central Pub.

Bridwell, Norman. 1985. *Clifford the Big Red Dog*. Scholastic

Britton, Andrew. 2006. *The American*. New York: Kensington Books

Brockes, Emma. 2008. *What Would Barbra Do? How Musicals Changed My Life*. Harper

Brown, C. Brene. 2012. *Daring Greatly*. New York, NY: Gotham Books

Buchanan, Missy. 2008. *Living with Purpose in a Worn-out Body*. Upper Room

Buder, Madonna. Sr. 2010. *Grace to Race*. New York: Simon & Schuster

Burke, James. 2007. *Tin Roof Blowdown*. Waterville, Me.: Wheeler Pub.

Burroughs, Augusten. 2012. *This is How*. Detroit: Thorndike Press

Byrne, J., 2012. *The Occupy Handbook*. Back Bay Books

Carr, Nicholas. 2010. *The Shallows: What the Internet is Doing to Our Brains*. New York: W.W. Norton

Carstensen, Laura. 2009. *Long Bright Future*. New York: Broadway Books

Cash, Wiley. 2012. *A Land More Kind than Home*. New York: William Morrow

Castelli, J., 1994. *How I Pray*. Ballantine Books

Chapman, Robin. and Judith Strasser, eds. 2007. *On Retirement: 75 Poems*. Iowa City: University of Iowa Press

Collins, Suzanne. 2008. *The Hunger Games*. New York: Scholastic Press

Claus, S., 2008. *Santa Responds He's Had Enough…and He's Writing Back!* Running Press

Dawson, George. 2000. *Life is so Good*. New York: Random House

Debaggio, Thomas. 2002. *Losing My Mind*. Waterville, Me.: Thorndike Press

Diamond, Jared. 2012. *The World Until Yesterday*. New York: Viking

Douglas-Klotz, Neil. 1990. *Prayers of the Cosmos*. San Francisco: Harper & Row

Dyer, Wayne. 2012. *Wishes Fulfilled*. Carlsbad, Ca.: Hay House

Endlich, Lisa. 2008. *Be the Change*. New York: Collins Business

Ephron, Nora. 2006. *I Feel Bad About My Neck*. New York: Random House

Evans, Richard. 2012. *The Road to Grace*. New York: Simon & Schuster

Evans, Richard. 2001. *The Christmas Box*. NewYork: Simon & Schuster

Feldman, David. 2000. *Imponderables*. New York: Galahad Books

Fischer, Ed. 2012. *You're Never Too Old to Laugh*. Meadowbrook

Fishman, Ted. 2010. *Shock of Gray*. New York: Scribner

Forman, Paula. 2009. *The Hour Glass Solution: A Boomer's Guide to the Rest of Your*
Life. Da Capo Lifelong Books

Genova, Lisa. 2011. *Left Neglected*. Waterville, Me.: Wheeler Pub.

Gibran, Kahlil, 1923. *The Prophet*. Knopf

Gould, John. 2000. *Tales from Rhapsody Home*. Chapel Hill, NC: Algonquin Books of Chapel Hill

Graham, Billy. 2012. *Nearing Home*. Waterville, Me.: Thorndike Press

Grahame, Kenneth. 2011. *The Wind in the Willows*. Franklin, Tenn.: Dalmation Press

Green, John. 2012. *The Fault in Our Stars*. Waterville, Me.: Thorndike Press

Gross, Matthew. 2012. *The Last Myth: What the Rise of Apocalyptic Thinking Tells Us About America*. Prometheus Books

Haddon, Mark. 2011. *The Curious Incident of the Dog in the Night*. Prince Frederick, MD: Recorded Books

Hale, Regina. 2006. *Red Hat Society: Acting their Age*. Thorndike, Me.: Center Point

Halpern, Susan. 2004. *Etiquette of Illness*. Waterville, Me.: Thorndike Press

Hammond, L. and B.J Gallagher. 2010. *Oil for Your Lamp*. Simple Truths.

Hays, Edward. 2012. *Pilate's Prisoner: A Passion Play*. Booklocker.com, Inc.

Heagle, John. 2010. *Justice Rising: The Emerging Biblical Vision.* Orbis Books

Heller, Jane. 2012. *You'd Better Not Die or I'll Kill You: A Caregiver's Survival Guide to*

Keeping You in Good Health and Good Spirits. Chronicle Books.

Heuertz,C. and Richard Rohr. 2013. *Unexpected Gifts: Discovering the Way of Community.* Howard Books

Hillenbrand, Laura. 2001. *Seabiscuit.* Random House Publishing Group

Hillman, James. 1999. *The Force of Character.* New York: Random House

Hitchens, Christopher. 2012. *Mortality.* New York: Twelve.

Housden, Roger. 2004. *Ten Poems to Last a Lifetime.* New York: Harmony Books

Jacobs, A.J. 2012. *Drop Dead Healthy.* Waterville, Me.: Thorndike Press

James, E.L. 2012. *Fifty Shades of Gray.* New York: Random House

James, Alison. 2004. *I Used to Miss Him.* Adams Media

Jenner, Paul. 2008. *Teach Yourself Happiness.* Blacklick, OH: McGraw-Hill Companies

Johnson, Barbara. 2009. *Humor Me I'm Over the Hill.* Thomas Nelson

Johnson, Barbara. 1997. *Living Somewhere Between Estrogen and Death.* Dallas, TX: Word Pub.

Johnson, Barbara. 2006. *Humor Me, I'm Your Mother.* Nashville, TN: W Pub. Group

Joyce, James. 1992. *Ulysses.* Random House, Inc.

Kingsberry, Karen. 2010. *Unlocked.* Detroit: Thorndike Press

Kisor, Henry. 2010. *What's That Pig Outdoors.* Urbana: University of Illinois Press

Lakin, Rita. 2007. *Getting Older is Criminal.* Waterville, Me.: Thorndike Press

Lamott, Anne. 2012. *Help, Thanks, Wow!* Waterville, Me.: Thorndike Press

Lawson, Jenny. 2012. *Let's Pretend This Never Happened.* New York: G.P. Putnam's Sons

Lehrer, Jonah. 2012. *Imagine.* Boston: Houghton Mifflin Harcourt.

Leviton, Daniel. 2008. *The World in Six Songs: How the Musical Brain Created Human*

Nature. New York: Dutton

Lindbergh, Anne. 2005. *Gift from the Sea*. New York: Pantheon

Lindbergh, Reeve. 2008. *Forward from Here*. New York: Simon & Schuster

Lindsey, Hal. 1970. *The Late Great Planet Earth*. Grand Rapids: Zondervan

Litwin, Eric. 2010. *Pete the Cat: I Love My White Shoes*. New York: Harper

Lufton, Robert. 2011. *Toxic Charity*. New York: HarperOne

Macy, Joanna. 2012. *Active Hope: How to Face the Mess*. Novato, Ca. New World

Library

Maloney, Stuart. 2011. *26*. Bloomington, IN: AuthorHouse

Manley, Brent. 2005. *The Tao of Bridge*. Adams Media

Martin, James. 2010. *The Jesuit Guide to Almost Everything*. New York: HarperOne

McKibben, Bill. 2005. *The Comforting Whirlwind: God, Job, and the Scale of Creation*.

Cowley Publications.

McWilliam, Candia. 2010. *What to Look for in Winter*. New York: HarperCollins

Merrifield, Andy. 2008. *The Wisdom of Donkeys*. New York: Walker & Company

Meyer, Joyce. 2010. *Power Thoughts*. New York: FaithWords

Milne, A.A. 2010. *Winnie-the-Pooh*. New York: Disney Press

Moggach, Deborah. 2012. *The Best Exotic Marigold Hotel*. Random House

Monaghan, Brian. 2009. *Power of Two*. New York: Workman Pub.

Montalvan, Luis. 2011. *Until Tuesday*. Waterville, Me.: Thorndike Press

Morgan, R. and Jane Marie Thibault. 2012. *Pilgrimage into the Last Third of Life: 7*

Gateways to Spiritual Growth. Upper Room

Naidoo, Beverly. 2011. *Aesop's Fables*. London: Francis Lincoln Children's Books

Nemtin, Ben. 2012. *Buried Life: What Do You Want to Do Before You Die?* New York: Artisan

Nimmer, Kathy. 2010. *Two Plus Four Equals One*. Indianapolis, IN: Dog Ear Pub.

Nouwen, Henri. 2009. *Bread for the Journey: A Daybook of Wisdom and Faith.*
HarperCollins
Nuland, Sherwin. 2007. *The Art of Aging.* New York: Random House
Oriah. 2009. *The Dance.* HarperCollins
Patterson, James. 2012. *Merry Christmas Alex Cross.* New York: Hachette
Patterson, James. 2011. *The Christmas Wedding.* North Kingstown, RI: AudioGO
Peacock, Molly. 2011. *The Paper Garden.* New York: Bloomsbury
Perry, John. 2012. *Art of Procrastination.* New York: Workman
Picoult, Jodi. 2010. *House Rules.* New York: Atria Books
Piper, Watty. 2012. *The Little Engine that Could.* Grosset & Dunlap
Quindlen, Anna. 2012. *Lots of Candles Plenty of Cake.* New York: Random House
Rand, Ayn. 2005. *The Fountainhead.* New York: Plume
Remen, Rachel Naomi. 2007. *Kitchen Table Wisdom.* New York: Riverhead Books
Rosen, L., I Disorder
Rubin, Gretchen. 2012. *Happier at Home: Kiss More, Jump More, Abandon a Project, Read Samuel Johnson, and My Other Experiments in the Practice of Everyday Life.* New York: Crown Archetype
Sankovitch, Nina. 2011. *Tolstoy and the Purple Chair.* Thorndike, Me.: Center Point Pub.
Sarton, May. 1984. *At Seventy.* New York: W.W. Norton
Sarton, May. 1995. *Endgame.* W.W. Norton & Co.
Satran, Pamela. 2009. *How Not to Act Old.* HarperCollins
Schneider, Katherine. 2010. *Your Treasure Hunt: Disabilities and Finding Your Gold.* Edina, MN: Beaver's Pond Press
Schneider, Katherine. 2005. *To the Left of Inspiration.* Indianapolis, IN: Dog Ear Publishing
Schoenfeld, Charles. 2011. *A Funny Thing Happened on My Way to the Dementia Ward:*
Memoir of a Male CNA. Stevens Point, WI: Schoenfeld
Schwalb, Will. 2012. *The End of Your Life Book Club.* New York: Alfred A. Knopf
Seger, Linda. 2006. *Jesus Rode a Donkey.* Avon, Mass.: Adams Media
Selznick, Brian. 2011. *Wonderstruck.* New York: Scholastic

Seo, Danny. 2012. *Upcycling*. Philadelphia, PA: Running Press

Seuss, Dr. 1986. *You're Only Old Once*. New York: Random House

Sheehy, Gail. 1995. *Passages*. Random House Publishing Group

Silverstein, Shel. 1992. *The Giving Tree*. New York: HarperCollins

Simonson, Helen. 2010. *Major Pettigrew's Last Stand*. New York: Random House

Slade, Giles. 2012. *The Big Disconnect*. Amherst, NY: Prometheus Books

Sleeth, M., 24/6

Smith, H. and Cynthia Darlow. 2005. *The Red Hat Club*. Thorndike, Me.: Center Point Pub.

Smith, Manuel. 1975. *When I Say "No" I Feel Guilty*. New York: Bantam

Somers, Suzanne. 2012. *Bombshell*. New York: Crown Archetype

Spiers, Peter. 2012. *Master Class: Living Longer, Stronger, and Happier*.

Srode, Molly. 2004. *Keeping Spiritual Balance as You Grow Older: More than 65 Creative Ways to Use Purpose, Prayer, and the Power of Spirit to Build a Meaningful Retirement*. Woodstock, VT: SkyLight Paths Pub.

St. Augustine, John. 2006. *Living an Uncommon Life: Essential Lessons from 21 Extraordinary People*. Hampton Roads.

Stegner, Wallace. 1988. *Crossing to Safety*. Thorndike, Me.: Thorndike Press

Stoddard, Alexandra. 2002. *Choosing Happiness : Keys to a Joyful Life*. New York: HarperCollins

Strobel, Tammy. 2012. *You Can Buy Happiness (and it's cheap:) How One Woman Radically Simplified Her Life and How You Can To .* Novato, CA: New World Library

Stroud, J Francis SJ. 2005. *Praying Naked: The Spirituality of Anthony de Mello*. Image

Sullivan, Tom. 2012. *As I See It*. Detroit, MI: Thorndike Press

Thayer, Nancy. 2006. *Hot Flash Club*. Thorndike, Me.: Center Point Pub.

Thoreau, Henry. 2004. *Walden*. Princeton University Press

Turkle, Sherry. 2011. *Alone Together*. New York: Basic Books

Twelftree, Graham. 2011. *The Cambridge Companion to Miracles (Cambridge Companions to Religion)*. Cambridge University Press

Verghese, Abraham. 2011. *Cutting for Stone*. Waterville, Me.: Thorndike Press

Warner, Carolyn. 2010. *The Words of Extraordinary Women*. William Morrow Books.

Warden, Bob. 2010. *Bob Warden's Slow Food Fast*. Dynamic Housewares

Wilder, Laura Ingalls. 1989. *Little House on the Prairie*. Santa Barbara, CA: Cornerstone Books

Wilkerson, Isabel. 2010. *The Warmth of Other Suns*. New York: Random House

Wilkinson, Bruce. 2009. *You were Born for This*. Colorado Springs, CO: Multnomah Books

Williams, Margery. 2012. *The Velveteen Rabbit*. Kennebunkport, Me.: Appleseed Press

Winterson, Jeanette. 2013. *Why Be Happy When You Can be Normal?* Grove Press

Witkin, Georgia. 1984. *The Female Stress Syndrome*. New York: Newmarket Press

Young, William. 2007. *The Shack*. Windblown Media

Zaleski, Philip. 2001. *Best American Spiritual Writing 2001*. Houghton Mifflin Harcourt Publishing Company

Zusak, Markus. 2006. *The Book Thief*. Perfection.

CPSIA information can be obtained at www.ICGtesting.com
Printed in the USA
LVOW07s2239090415

434017LV00003B/204/P